ART CRAFT AND DESIGN

IN THE PRIMARY SCHOOL

Edited by John Lancaster

NATIONAL SOCIETY FOR EDUCATION IN ART & DESIGN

CONTENTS

CHAPTER 6   SUPPLEMENTARY MATERIAL

CHAPTER 7   MATERIALS

CHAPTER 8   BIBLIOGRAPHY

PREFACE

In 1983 the National Society for Art Education decided to set up a working party to prepare some 'Guidelines for teachers' of art, craft and design in the Primary School. This task was undertaken only after much soul-searching because it was felt that such documents were diminished in value if they were not supported by substantial in-service training courses. Indeed some members of the working party believed at the outset that curriculum developments of this kind were of real value only to those teachers fortunate enough themselves to be members of a working party investigating guidelines. However, at an early stage in the Project the Society received over 40 sets of primary art guidelines mainly prepared on the initiative of local authority art advisers. Plotting the territory covered by these often excellent documents on a map of the United Kingdom provided convincing evidence that there was a need for a national publication, if only because almost three-quarters of the map remained unshaded. The Society overcame its doubts, believing that it had a duty to do something to meet a pressing need rather than wait for action to be taken by others. This book is the outcome.

The working party benefited from the contribution made by members of the Society for Education through Art (S.E.A.) and the National Society for Art Education (N.S.A.E.) and when these groups merged to form the National Society for Education in Art and Design (N.S.E.A.D.), in October 1984, the new Society continued with the project strengthened by the addition of new members. The members of the working party — who offered a wide range of experience — are listed on the *Acknowledgements* page. All made a valuable contribution to the final draft but perhaps particular mention should be made of the following individuals who worked closely together to produce the final draft:

> Bob Clement
> Liz Cotton
> Ivan Davies
> Gill Figg
> Dr John Lancaster (Editor & Research Officer).

I believe that members of the NSEAD and all primary school teachers, and perhaps their Head-Teachers and LEA primary advisers, who have the opportunity to study this book will owe the joint authors a considerable debt of gratitude.

John Steers
NSEAD General Secretary
June 1986

ACKNOWLEDGEMENTS

Many people helped me by endless discussion, by phoning and writing and by criticising and correcting drafts of this book. I thank them and the Primary Art Working Party of primary teachers, primary head-teachers, H.M.I., art advisers, art and design teachers, teacher-education tutors, heads of teachers' centres and NSEAD officers, for their work on behalf of the Society. They are:

Professor Brian Allison	Ray Haslam
Bob Clement	David Holt
Liz Cotton	Kay Howard-Harris
Ivan Davies (Chairman)	Alastair Laing
Dr. Anthony Dyson	Roy Prentice
Mavis Eccles	Peter Riches
Nigel Edmondson	David Sharples
Gillian Figg	David Williams
John Fulton HMI	Peter Woolley
Daniel Gleeson	Mrs K. J. Tambling

It is important to state that the support which the Society has received from *John Storrs*, media relations manager, Berol Ltd., in Kings Lynn, Norfolk, and the sponsorship of that company, have been invaluable to the success of the project and a strong appreciation must be recorded. Thanks are also due to a number of individuals for their special contributions, including *Eileen Adams* (Royal College of Art — written materials); *Ian G Bliss* (St Martin's College, Lancaster — criticism); *John Broomhead* (a Devon Secondary School — curriculum development group material); *John Davie* (College of St Paul & St Mary, Cheltenham — photographs); *Owen Eardley* (South Glamorgan Institute of Higher Education, Cardiff — photographs); *Joan Gaunt* (once a teacher and then Senior Tutor for Early Childhood Education in a college of education — reading, criticism and correction of the preliminary draft); *Ron George* (Bretton Hall College of Higher Education, Wakefield — illustrative materials); *Margaret Harvey* (Head-teacher in Avon — school work and written material concerned with 3D design-related activities); *Katie Macleod* (Museum Service Officer — museum-based ideas); *Elizabeth Tarr*; *Alison Brachtogel* (for her junior school outline structure); *Arthur Hughes & colleagues* (Birmingham Polytechnic — comments on art in a multi-racial society); *Ralph Jeffery,* formerly Staff Inspector; *Guy Scott,* (art teacher, lecturer and artist); *Michael Stevenson* (Curriculum Development Leader for the Visual Arts, Manchester LEA — assessment profile); *Margaret Morgan* (Art Adviser, Suffolk County Council — permission to quote from that county's art guidelines); *as well as Jacci Cawte, Anne Ingall, Tony Charlton* (Research Assistant) and *John Steers* (General Secretary) for their help and support at the NSEAD Head Office in Corsham; thanks also go to the many LEAs who sent copies of their art guidelines to the Society. Finally, a word of appreciation must be given to those schools and young children (they know who they are) who contributed to this document both wittingly and unwittingly.

John Lancaster.

John Lancaster
Editor

INTRODUCTION

Reputable schemes of work exist in most subject areas, including *art, craft and design*, but if an individual school has not formulated an art curriculum policy, class teachers are left very much to their own devices. Few primary school teachers would claim to be specialists, for the nature of their work is such that they have responsibility across the whole curriculum, and while many are strongly sympathetic to art and teach it with enthusiasm, there tends to be a need for some guidance and support.

It is hoped that this book will prove a valuable source of reference for teachers and head-teachers while making a positive contribution to the quality of art, craft and design education in primary schools. It must be pointed out at the outset that teachers need not be artistically talented in order to teach the subject with sensitivity and imagination. Indeed, those who consider themselves to be talented, in an artistic sense, may find it difficult, at first, to work easily with young children. Artistic ability on the part of the teacher is no substitute for skilful teaching. The teacher applies the same skills in art, craft and design lessons as in other areas of the curriculum. With sufficient confidence, the teacher can encourage pupils to transcend their own artistic competence by providing appropriate stimuli, materials and conditions for learning. It will be appreciated that this applies as much to the art lesson as to the science lesson: it is "discovery" work, and its parameters need not be restricted by the teacher's existing knowledge of the subject. Difficulties arise from the fact that the primary school teacher is expected to be an expert in all areas of the curriculum. A flexible approach to teaching the subject is wise and the following points may help to define the teacher's role in ensuring that pupils are given every opportunity to develop their art and design skills. Teachers should:

1. provide, in co-operation with colleagues, a school environment which is an encouragement to visual learning;
2. create, as part of such an environment, well-planned spaces abounding with interesting man-made and natural stimuli (*Art in Junior Education* published by the DES in 1978 illustrates this well);
3. plan practical activity areas in which good quality art materials and tools are within easy reach and can be used safely;
4. stimulate ideas and discussion among pupils, while also giving encouragement and generating worthwhile artistic learning experiences in which ideas are shared;
5. guide their pupils' decision-making sensitively so that children are supported (and intellectually stretched when this is appropriate) in seeking personal solutions to problems in art, craft and design;
6. instruct pupils in the correct and safe use of tools and equipment, and in the handling of materials;
7. develop learning experiences which provide opportunities for pupils to engage in personal programmes of work as well as in co-operative schemes with other pupils.

Many of the LEA art guidelines which exist support these points, while art advisers and teachers' working parties throughout the country demonstrate a large measure of agreement on fundamental philosophical and practical criteria.

It is also commonly agreed that the attitude of a school and, in particular, of an individual teacher to the role of art in the education of the young child probably has a strong bearing on the pupil's own attitude to art activities and, as a result, on the quality of the learning experiences. It is important to understand that well-considered art programmes assist the child's intellectual and aesthetic development while also providing a means for visual communication and expression. The pupil learns through his senses and therefore art activities draw upon sensory experiences crucial to the child's educational development and fundamental to the school curriculum. What children learn of the world through their senses has to be structured in terms of language, or in the form of images, if it is to be regarded as "usable knowledge". Children's senses are very acute and they need appropriate materials and activities to give *form* to their experiences and *order* to their ideas. Image-making and language are closely related. Young children are often more articulate through their picture-making than through their writing, although both means of expression are vital to the primary curriculum and essential to the development of learning.

The teacher can help by providing an appropriately-structured art, craft and design programme, and it is hoped that the ideas and materials presented here will be helpful in this respect. These suggestions are certainly not intended to be definitive, but to be developed to suit individual circumstances. This publication intends to encourage and guide teachers to provide their pupils with the best possible art, craft and design education. Above all, we hope it will help class teachers to develop their own curriculum-planning and teaching styles with confidence. *Our aims may be summarised as follows:*

1. to communicate basic information about art, craft and design education to the primary school teacher;
2. to promote the aims and philosophies of art, craft and design in primary schools, and to advise on content and practice; and
3. to encourage all concerned with the education of young children to extend and build on present thinking and practice.

Good practice where it is observed, whether by members of the NSEAD, HMI or LEA advisers, can be recognised, understood and described. The intention of this document is to describe the kind of provision which supports good practice and to indicate how levels of provision might generally be improved. The primary teacher is invited to use this book with sensitivity and commonsense, seeing it as a starting point and an aid to thoughtful educational practice which has the interest of the child as its core.

ART, CRAFT & DESIGN

Modern trends in the education of young children in their primary schools have, to a great extent, evolved from Hadow's recommendations in the early 1930s regarding 'activity' methods and 'first-hand experience' (Hadow Report 1931). Handicrafts and art — often thought of in the past in terms of simple basketry, raffia work, bookbinding or drawing and painting with pencils, pens, crayons and powder colours — have, traditionally, been seen as separate curriculum subjects. In the 1980s, however, art, craft and design, because of their inter-relationship — have tended to be grouped even closer together. Artists and craftspersons are also designers and it is therefore unhelpful to consider these activities in isolation when children are involved in art. Indeed, art is also considered an 'aesthetic' subject and, as such, has links with music, dance and drama.

CREATIVITY is central to art, craft and design activity and is an attribute equivalent to intelligence. It involves the expression of personal ideas in an original and sensitive manner.

ART is a 'creative' process encompassing expression, observation, communication and appraisal, and is generally associated with painting and sculpture.

CRAFT is concerned with the processes and techniques of designing and use of materials in the manual arts with skilled craftsmanship.

DESIGN is that area of inventive, artistic activity concerned with prescribing form, structure or pattern for a proposed man-made artifact or work of art, and depends upon acquired knowledge, analytical and practical skills and decision-making.

The terms *art, craft* and *design* are used repeatedly throughout this publication. In the main, however, the terms are combined to embrace *one* broad curricular area. It is clear that:

ART, CRAFT & DESIGN together form that range of work with both two- and three-dimensional materials which is often known as 'creative activities' of 'art and crafts'.

It normally includes the acquisition of some traditional craft skills as well as independent pupil-directed work and group work. In addition to work separately time-tabled it takes in the use of drawing and model-making as major means of learning across the curriculum.
This aspect of the curriculum provides an important base of experience upon which aesthetic, scientific and technological insights can be built.
The arts have been among the most potent forces in the development and shaping of our culture and its traditions . . . to have an informed and appreciative grasp of the growth and tenor of our civilisation, our children must have some awareness and understanding of the principal forms of creation and communication in which its development may be most sharply discerned — the world of the arts.
(*The Arts in Schools*, Calouste Gulbenkian Foundation Report, 1982, page 21 para 17)
THE AESTHETIC AND CREATIVE area is concerned with the capacity to respond emotionally and intellectually to sensory experience; the awareness of degrees of quality; and the appreciation of beauty and fitness for purpose. It involves the exploration

and understanding of feeling and the processes of making, composing and inventing. Aesthetic and creative experience may occur in any part of the curriculum, but some subjects contribute particularly to the development of pupils' aesthetic awareness and understanding because they call for personal, imaginative, effective, and often practical, responses to sensory experience. Art, crafts, design, some aspects of technology, music, dance, drama and theatre arts, in particular, promote the development of the imagination and the creative use of media and materials.

(DES, *The Curriculum from 5 to 16* (Curriculum Matters 2), HMSO, 1985, para 36)

1

ART, CRAFT & DESIGN
IN THE
PRIMARY SCHOOL

5. Why we need to teach art, craft & design in the primary school.

Art, craft and design (taken together as one curricular area) serves many functions in the primary schools. It provides rigorous creative experiences with materials and art forms; and it can also complement other curricular activities by acting as a stimulus for subject studies while inter-relating these through display, illustration and presentation. It also feeds into drama, in the form of costume design, the designing of sets and publicity — i.e. posters, tickets and programmes, make-up, as well as impinging upon rituals and festivals.

All pupils should experience the 'aesthetic and creative' area of learning. It is suggested, however, that this should not be seen as a discrete element to be taught separately and in isolation from other parts of the curriculum. Indeed, HMI state that areas of learning and experience should not be equated with particular subjects for, they point out, 'pupils may gain scientific or mathematical experience from art, and aesthetic experience from mathematics' (DES *The Curriculum from 5-16* (Curriculum Matters 2), HMSO, 1985, para 33).

Opportunities for experimenting, enquiring, designing and making permit children to use materials expressively. In doing so they should be encouraged to use a range of materials inventively. There will, however, be occasions when the children's work will be developed to meet requirements of a functional nature — for instance, when they apply craft skills in textiles or claywork, or the designing of posters or books. Involvement in the visual and plastic arts should inspire self-confidence and imaginative identification with the culture in which both teachers and children live.

Children like to draw, paint, write, print, dance and sing. In other words they like to make things and to be creative.

It is therefore essential that all children should have opportunities to explore the elements of art. These included *colour, line, shape, form, tone, texture, pattern* and *arrangement,* so that they may acquire a basic grammar of visual form and, through personal experience and development, an increased aesthetic awareness and knowledge of design.

It is important that teachers recognise the value of linking such studies with the observation of 'real' things.

Good classroom practice will enable children to be involved in making art, looking at, thinking about, feeling about, knowing about and responding to art, craft and design.

If the aims of education are in part to give pupils a sense of excellence and quality in human achievement, then clearly arts teaching will have a central part to play in this.
(From *The Arts in Schools*, Calouste Gulbenkian Foundation Report, 1982, page 21 para 18)

If artistic experiences are to feed the imagination they need to be personal encounters in which children are encouraged to think and act independently. Pupils must also be given time to complete work in a satisfying way, as well as being encouraged to consider it critically with personal discrimination.

This subject area certainly provides a means by which children can be adventurous and thoughtful individuals and will give them the chance to learn through a variety of purposeful activities. It is important that we should aim to educate young children to look at the world with curiosity and to respond to the environment with concern and understanding. So we must ensure that as an inter-related part of the curriculum, art, craft and design is not concerned only with producing drawings, paintings and functional objects, but provides an education in which children can develop into well-informed, intelligent observers and critics.

The planning of an art, craft and design curriculum can commence by thinking about what young children might be expected to do during their primary schooling (i.e. 5-11 years), for this will form a useful framework for the teacher who is seeking to structure a sensitive and purposeful curriculum. It is essential that children should have opportunities to learn from practical experience in both *two-* and *three*-dimensional work.

TWO-DIMENSIONAL WORK will help primary pupils:
- to draw and paint confidently, expressively and with enjoyment;
- to understand and to represent two-dimensional shapes and to indicate proportions;
- to understand and represent three-dimensional space;
- to recognise and represent differences in line, form, texture, tone and colour from direct observation;
- to recognise and explore some characteristic differences of materials and media;
- to understand how to relate parts to the whole in developing composition;

A 'play' structure for a young child made by two Primary teachers on an in service course.

- to recognise and delight in familiar patterns and to discern and invent new ones;
- to understand the major colour relationships and differences; and
- to recognise and respond to differences in atmosphere and mood;
- to learn about the characteristics of yarns, fabrics and threads and their use in sewing, weaving, knitting, cutting and assembling; and
- to use the characteristics of such materials to represent differences and qualities observed in natural and man-made forms.

THREE-DIMENSIONAL WORK will enable young children:
- to understand something of the relationships between form, function and material upon which design and craftsmanship are founded;
- to experience and better understand the characteristics of and enjoyment in using resistant and plastic materials such as card, wood, metal, stone, clay, wire, yarns and plaster in constructing, carving, modelling and moulding;
- to observe, understand and represent three-dimensional forms and relationships; and
- to use models to simulate real or imagined situations and to help solve problems.

EXPERIENCE OF ART, CRAFT AND DESIGN WORKS will enable children to:
—recognise different approaches taken by artists, craftsmen and designers in their work.
—appreciate the different forms art, craft and design can take and the various purposes which they serve.
—recognise that art, craft and design differs from culture to culture.
—be able to talk and express their ideas and feelings about art, craft and design work.
—acquire a verbal vocabulary which will allow them to talk about, art, craft and design in a critical as well as a personal way.

6. What primary-age pupils should have experienced or achieved in art, craft and design before moving to the secondary school.

Art, craft and design in the Primary School makes a fundamental contribution to children's education which continues at least until the end of formal education in adolescence and, often, beyond into adulthood. Although art, craft and design activity in the Primary School has particular characteristics and provides experiences which are essentially related to the early years of children's growth and development, it is very important to see it as part of a sequential whole in which learning and experience is cumulative. Indeed, as is the case with all aspects of the curriculum, what is done in the early years of schooling lays the foundation for all subsequent educational experience.

There is general agreement on the overall aims of art, craft and design education, to which activities at all ages and stages should relate, and these can be summed up as follows:
1. The development of a broad understanding of the meaning, significance and contributions of art, craft and design in contemporary culture;
2. The development of perceptual skills leading to a sensitivity to visual and tactile qualities, together with an enhancement of experience in art, craft and design;
3. The development of informed aesthetic judgement, both in personal terms and in the community;
4. The ability to value and experience meaningfully the cultural heritage of this and other societies, past and present;
5. The ability to be able to hold, articulate and communicate ideas, opinions and feelings about art, craft and design;
6. The development of particular individual subject aptitudes and interest, but not exclusively in production and expression.

The activities implicit in these aims could be taken to include making, looking at, thinking about, talking about, feeling about, knowing about and responding to art, craft and design. The achievement of these aims would be dependent on the formation of a range of fundamental concepts regarding the nature of art, craft and design. (NSAE, 1978. *Schools Council 'N & F' Proposals*)

Another way of visualising these aims is for children to be helped — through their art, craft and design activities, study and discussions — to obtain:
- personal accomplishment;
- a heightened consciousness of the part played by the subject in present-day societies; and
- a comprehension of the importance of art, craft and design to the culture which they have inherited

These general aims, which really can be considered as the purposes of art, craft and design activities in the primary school, need to be borne in mind in following through the remainder of this volume.

In the course of their school-work children will develop a range of practical expertise arising through individual and group activity. They will use the skills which they have learnt to examine and explore objects and events of interest to them and these will, typically, include *family, school* and *community events, places* visited, *objects* and *phenomena observed* (e.g. natural forms, structures and parts of plants; small and large creatures; people and costume; *buildings and other man-made devices and equipment*), as well as *enriched and changed environments* supporting festivals and dramatic events. Such work will go right across the school curriculum while inter-relating all manner of learning experiences.

7. An education in art, craft and design at primary level will ensure that children:

- know that they can directly affect the quality of the man-made environment by what they contribute to it, by way of images, forms and artifacts;
- can recognise and represent broad differences of character and feeling;
- experience the satisfaction to be derived from both individual and co-operative manufacture;
- have learnt to persist in overcoming perceptual and technical difficulties;
- are able to use a basic vocabulary of criticism;
- have seen and handled, where appropriate, original works and know something of their origin;
- have first-hand knowledge of their cultural heritage as it is represented in their locality and recognise some of the characteristics of more distant or different cultures;
- have learnt to draw and to make models with confidence and have an understanding of various methods of representation;
- understand how art, craft and design skills such as drawing, mapping, and model-making assist the study of subjects such as history, geography, science and mathematics.

Although much of the work will be of a practical nature it should be remembered that discussion with the children about *making things* and *looking at things* is an essential element of any curriculum in the expressive and creative arts. This balances their own involvement in designing and craftsmanship, both as 'thinkers' and 'makers', for their involvement in artistic work engages children in consideration of design problems.

(See 'An approach to 3D art and design-related activities with infants in Chapter 3).

8. The stages of artistic development up to the age of eleven?

If we have an understanding of the broad stages of development and the main characteristics of the graphic imagery which children produce, our planning of art, craft and design teaching/learning programmes and stategies will be greatly enhanced. What we give here as a general guide is a simplified sequence in the belief that teachers will already be aware of the various stages, ages and characteristics.

The Suffolk County Council's guidelines *Art in the First Years of Schooling: 4-11* (p15) indentifies five basic modes in which children work:

1. *Experimentation and Experience of Materials and Tools*
   (——18 months-18 years——)
2. *Symbolic Interpretation*
   In the early years (——3-7/8 year——) it will be based on holistic scanning and global vision. Later it can continue into adult years as a valid option for communication and expression.
3. *Predominantly Symbolist Approach*
   (——5-12 years——) Showing a growing interest in a variety of items and a complexity of images, together with the appearance of a visual/analytic approach in parts of the work.
4. *Predominantly Analytic Approach*
   (——7/8 years—— onwards) The need for visual realism is paramount. Matching and comparisons are important, but symbolist overtones will often be apparent.
5. *Analytic Approach*
   (——8/9 years—— onwards) Visual realism based on personal experience through the senses and interpreted through the use of a variety of media.

These five modes are inter-related and take us through to the end of the junior stage. Teachers often note, however, that exceptionally gifted children in the infant school are capable of and even get involved in aspects of other developmental stages, while older children and even adults will need to revert to the earlier stages as a means of 'repeating' experiences or of strengthening them. The developmental pattern of children's image making cannot be strictly sequential because any individual child's development may not correspond directly with proposed stages. Indeed, no child fits into a prescribed pattern exactly and this should therefore be seen as a generalisation which it is hoped will give rise to thoughtful discussion and planning.

- SCRIBBLING AND DRAWING
  (from early infancy)
  — exploration through sensory experiences
  — broad physical movements
  — accidental mark-making and freely-made imagery
  — play activities important

- SYMBOLISM
  (pre-school, infant and early junior)
  — less apparent random mark-making
  — variations introduced
  — image-making developing more control
  — more considered selection of shapes, forms and colours
  — representational elements more in evidence
  — observation more apparent
  — physical control increasing

- SCHEMATIC
  (mid to top junior)
  — increasing emphasis on realism through personal experience
  — more logically-conceived and analysed shapes
  — constructive building of objects and models
  — co-operative group work used increasingly as a working mode
  — work increasingly representational
  — design consciousness awakening
  — increasing interest in technology and analysis.

A particular value stressed in the Suffolk *guidelines* is the teacher's ability to show pupils that 'different' ways of looking and working are not inherently better or worse than others. Pupils need to see how the different methods are used by adults (see page 26 in the Suffolk C.C. *guidelines* which is an important follow-up to these stages).

It must be recognised, of course, that visual perception and forms of representation, such as in drawing, are very much conditioned by the children's cultural backgrounds. For some children from non-European backgrounds, the stages of drawing development described here do not apply, particularly in relation to drawing from observation. The teacher in the multicultural classroom needs to be very sensitive to the different views of art, craft and design which are held by ethnic minority communities represented in the school.

9. Art across the curriculum.

Primary teachers, as 'all-rounders' concerned with the broad curriculum, can often plan work to include visual and creative experiences within a variety of subject areas. In any consideration of the collaborative potential of art, craft and design it is important to recognise the contribution made by this aspect of children's learning to their development as individuals, otherwise there is a danger that the art activity done in association with other curriculum work can be a superficial time and space-filling exercise.

A multitude of ideas abound within the basic primary school curriculum and the local environment which can act as starting points for a range of artistic activities which may in turn lead into other curriculum areas. Two related approaches could be:

(1) a consideration of opportunities existing in other areas of the curriculum for enriching children's artistic and aesthetic experiences and for contributing to the aims of art, craft and design; and

(2) an exploration of the ways in which art, craft and design can contribute to children's learning in other curriculum areas.

Matthew Green

Zoe

If children observe the constructional patterns in timber-framed buildings through their drawings and photographs, they can go on to develop paintings, prints and models. In doing so, their work will be related to architecture, history, art, craft design and mathematics and they will be much more aware of art in the built environment.

Robert

TEACHERS AND PUPILS

10. Teacher/pupil relationships

1. What are our attitudes to children's experience of life and to the opinions and ideas which they derive from it?
2. What *positive* importance do we attach to building and maintaining self-images so that individual children can develop qualities of *confidence, responsibility, curiosity, tolerance* and *understanding*?

These questions affect our teaching and as they are particularly relevant to the teaching of art, craft and design they can form the basis for useful discussion with colleagues.

●DO WE VALUE CHILDREN'S EXPERIENCE?

Each child has a different experience of life in which some aspects are unique while others may be commonplace. This might lead us to ask such further questions as:

1. What child experiences can we draw upon in our art, craft and design teaching so that these are shared?
2. How can we weave these into our curriculum planning?
3. What kind of learning situations can we structure so that children can extend their range of experiences in a personal way?
4. How can pupils bring knowledge gained from their experiences to bear upon problems and judgements about design?
5. What experiences of tools, materials and skills can we provide as an extension of their experiences?

●DO WE VALUE CHILDREN'S OPINIONS AND IDEAS?

As we plan our art, craft and design teaching, therefore, we might ask ourselves:

1. Do we value children's ideas and opinions enough?
2. How can we equate our own and the children's ideas and points of view?
3. How can we develop the ideas of *different* children within a class and also throughout a school?
4. How might we and our pupils respond to *shared* opinions and ideas?

●ARE WE SUFFICIENTLY AWARE OF THE CHILD'S SELF-IMAGE

What we all think and feel about ourselves constitutes our 'self-image'. This image is made up of what we perceive to be true about ourselves together with what we perceive to be other people's assessment of us by the things they say and by the ways in which they behave toward us.

Some further questions we might consider about:

●ART, CRAFT & DESIGN AND CHILDREN'S EXPERIENCE

— What use are we asking children to make of their experience?
— What do they notice?
— What do they collect?
— What things do they wish to bring to school?
— What do they remember?
— What can they draw, paint or make from memory?
— What things do they need to look at again?
— What places do they need to re-visit?
— How can we display or look at their work in ways that enable children to share experiences confidently?
— What experiences can pupils share with artists and craftsmen?
— How can their own use of materials help them to understand why and how artists and designers work?
— What about progression and challenge?

●ART, CRAFT & DESIGN AND CHILDREN'S OPINIONS

— What does children's work reveal to us about what and how they think?
— Is their style of drawing tentative and gentle or assertive and confident?
— Do they notice details or general atmosphere?
— Can they distinguish between one style and another in the work of adults or their peers?
— Are they aware of qualities as well as objects?
— Can they name them?
— Are they aware of their own preferences and those of other children in the class?
— Can they enjoy comparing things and looking at and talking about their similarities and differences?

●ART, CRAFT & DESIGN AND CHILDREN'S SELF-ESTEEM

— The history of art and design shows us that although we see and think differently there is also much that we can share. What uses, therefore, can we make of examples of works of art which can help pupils to have confidence in their own perceptions?
— What use do we make of pupils' ideas and opinions?
— How are these made evident in the environment?

11. The role of the head-teacher

Head-teachers are conscious that in striving to maintain a rational balance of 'academic' and 'social' learning in their schools, the artistic subjects should play a vital role in the all-round development of children. One head-teacher, *who encourages teachers to use art, craft and design as a core for all the learning taking place in her school*, writes in a personal way about her own role. 'I am', she says, 'the head of a *group 6 First School*, in an urban area, with three hundred and fifty children aged 5-9 years and a teaching staff of eleven. She continues:

I see my role as that of watching to see that all those in the school — both children and adults — no matter what their age or job may be, have every chance to develop towards their full potential in as many aspects of life as possible. It is important that the adults in the school, myself included, should see each day as a chance to learn something new while providing us with the opportunity to share with others something already experienced or something which might well be experienced. I have found that when a school has, at its heart, the excitement of continual discovery and a constant quest to master new skills then each child and adult gains as a person.

A caring attitude is something I aim for — that is, caring for each other, caring for any article or animal loaned to us, caring about our behaviour, especially when not being supervised, and caring about the quality of work we produce. In my experience this provides the 'right' kind of atmosphere for personal development to take place.

The environment we create throughout the school helps tremendously with all of these aims and is something I personally work hard at in order to set standards within the school. I believe that the extra care taken in the setting-up of learning situations, in the displaying of the children's work and in an attractive organisation of a classroom is then reflected in the care the children take with their own tasks and is certainly reflected in their behaviour. Having established the 'right' relationships and a 'good' environment within the school, as head, it is important that I watch the progression of each aspect of the curriculum. Where members of staff realise that everyone is still learning they are less worried about admitting difficulties, and where people are used to caring for each other then the sharing of ideas and expertise becomes a natural follow-on. With young children I think it is important to bear in mind the skills and concepts that we, as teachers, are trying to impart rather than laying down a body of knowledge to be learned. There are a lot of different areas of the curriculum we are asked to introduce in the primary school but when one analyses the fundamental skills beneath each they are mostly developments of perceptual skills, and such skills are all best taught through first-hand experiences. *Hence observation, in its widest application, that is through all the senses, is the corner-stone of education in our school.* We introduce the children to *close observation* as soon as they start school, encouraging them *to look and look again.* The more a child is encouraged to really look at, touch and talk about the things he is going to draw, the more detailed his work will be and the deeper his own knowledge will be. If, for instance, a child is drawing a picture of his house, depending on his age and developmental level, we would ask questions such as:

(a) Is there anything on the front door? If so, can you add it to your picture?

(b) Can you see the curtains from the outside? How are they patterned? Is there anything on the window sills?

(c) How are the bricks arranged? Is the pattern the same all the way up the wall?

(d) What pattern do the tiles make on the roof? Does anything stick out of the roof?

(e) How is the guttering fixed? Can you show this on your picture?

It is essential that children have the real thing to refer to and that the teacher is at hand to ask relevant and searching questions. This will encourage, perhaps demand, looking again and noticing more, so that the child's natural inquisitiveness is heightened.

With the older children we may also point out the difference in texture between, say, the roughness of the bricks and the smoothness of the painted areas and encourage them *to experiment* with soft pencils, charcoal, paints, glues or other materials. Through this each child will begin to find the best way of representing what he or she sees, feels and knows. We try to give our children a wide range of things to *handle, observe* and *work from* so that with the teacher's participation they will become aware of, for example:—

- the colour, shape and smell of a flower
- the pattern and structure of a spider's web
- the smoothness of metal
- the intricacy of the inside of a clock and the arrangement of its cog wheels (even the way it works in relation to the concept of 'time')
- the colours, textures and patterns of burnt rubbish
- the texture of bark on a tree
- the patterns and colours of a mackerel
- the skeletal arrangements of a fish's bones
- the shape of a snail
- the different surfaces we walk on in the playground, on the pavement, on grass or on hard mud
- the patterns and colours in the sky
- the roundness of an orange
- the wonder of pollen seen through a stereo-microscope

The photomicrograph (a photographic enlargement) below is a piece of polystyrene. The cellular structure of this material is clearly-seen and evokes a real sense of wonder and inquisitiveness.

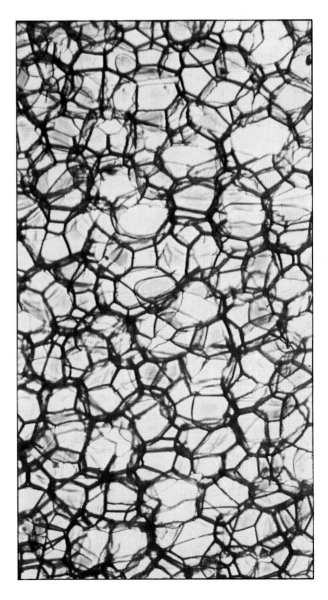

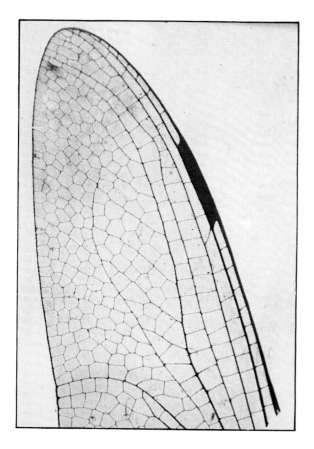

Linear patterns in an insect's wing (photography by Douglas Lawson). In looking at such forms pupils might notice ways in which they remind them of geometric shapes, architectural structures, re-inforcement engineering, traffic systems, urban maps, textures, light and shadow.

This print from a rubber mat was made by an eight-year-old girl.

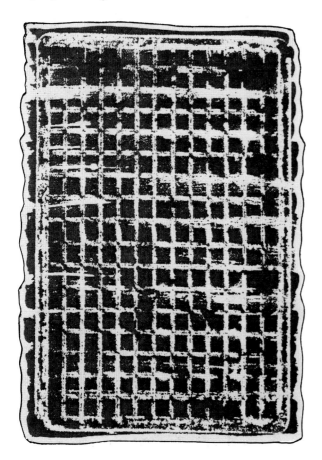

These are but a few of the visual and tactile experiences available to us for the wealth of material around us is limitless. But as adults we must continue to develop our own sensitivities as well as those of our pupils. Actually in our school we find that the children's comments help us 'to see' afresh! The normal child's sense of touch, smell, hearing and sight is very acute and my staff and I try to incorporate and extend these natural aptitudes so that the child's conception of the world around him is enhanced. We have found that as he becomes more aware of *pattern, structure, texture, shape and colour,* he is better able to produce imaginative work of depth because he has many internalised ideas upon which to draw; also, he will know how to use, adapt and incorporate the many resources around him.

As a head-teacher with no art training, I have found, through watching and listening to children that they learn best when using their full gamut of observational skills to:

1. develop more accurate language concepts;
2. become more aware of shape and colour;
3. be more ready to notice texture, pattern and design;
4. be less willing to make judgements on first impressions;
5. be better at devising ways of testing and extending findings;
6. be able to deal with more than one variable at a time;
7. be better able to choose the most appropriate materials, tools and media for the interpretation of a theme; and
8. be building up an inner store of experiences, patterns and designs that will be a source for their own creativeness.

12. Managing art in the classroom

The primary school teacher's job embraces a number or roles which obviously vary according to the age-groups and abilities of the pupils being taught. Many of the roles will not be concerned directly with the actual task of teaching, but they will certainly co-ordinate and unify the education of the pupil on an everyday, weekly and termly basis.

As far as art, craft and design education is concerned, *the teacher should plan the classroom environment as a lively and rich resource which will stimulate active interest.* This space and what it contains provide the main resources for learning by pupils in a particular class. In making decisions about what the space shall provide and about its form, its shape and its position the teacher uses judgements like those used by artists, architects and designers. Designing the space in which children will work requires forethought, inventiveness, a certain boldness, energy and a willingness to learn from experience. As in all design activity it is as well to start from an understanding of the constraints.

●TAKING STOCK

What can be changed and what must inevitably remain?
Most teachers inherit a classroom which has already been designed by its previous occupant for purposes broadly similar to their own. The new teacher will find it helpful to 'read' the existing design of the classroom.
What is the meaning or intended function of its layout?
How do these differ from the intentions of the new teacher?
What kind of messages does it convey to pupils?

The siting of the teacher's desk, for instance, on a raised platform has a functional advantage in that all the pupils can easily be seen by the teacher. It may also imply that the teacher is the central person in the classroom in whom all authority lies. An alternative positioning of the teacher's desk, say in a corner or at the side of the classroom, may indicate that the teacher rarely uses it as a position from which to address the class. Such a placing may indicate that the teacher expects to be more mobile and intends that the pupils should regard him/her as a consultant ready to share in the learning enterprises of the class, where 'authority' lies mainly in the nature of the work in hand. Similar considerations may govern the position of pupils' workplaces. These may serve either to separate or to group the pupils, to encourage mobility or stability according to the teacher's assessment of their learning needs.

With regard to *form and space* in the primary classroom, teachers might find it helpful to think-out a plan for an art, craft and design activities area which is sensibly organised. In such an area 3D materials and paints would ideally be separated from 2D materials.

(see plan on facing page).

● *Graphics/Drawing/Design* might occupy a central position and could contain *pencils, charcoal, pastels, crayons, inks, pens* etc.

● *Painting* would contain as wide a range as possible of powder and other types of paints and metallic gold and silver. Paint could be in small pots so that children could take them to other parts of the classroom on trays. Brushes, jars, pallettes, adhesives and other tools would be in this area.

● *Printmaking* might be located in the positions shown here — offering children experiences in some or all of the following — *mono-printing, finger printing, lino-printing* (top juniors), *potato (vegetable) printing, polyblock printing, screen printing, junk printing* and *fabric printing*.

● *3D/Collage* would take-up the remaining space and would include:

Clay — in a claybin in its plastic state — dried clay in another bin for reconstitution — tools to roll, slap, mould, impress, coil

Wood — a range of scrap pieces, balsa, cardboard off-cuts, etc., a saw, hammer, nails and sandpaper

Papier Mâché — newspaper, paste and two or three buckets

Wire — some thin and thicker types (fine/soft) and pliers

Junk — toilet rolls, polystyrene packing material, tins, plastic containers, bottle tops, cardboard boxes, etc.

Collage — papers, magazines, fabric, wallpapers, wrapping papers, threads and wools.

Classrooms vary in size and shape depending on whether they are in old, nineteenth century or modern purpose-built schools, and so these suggestions will require individual modification according to specific circumstances. Sometimes the children will suggest good ideas and class discussion may improve the working environment and help to solve difficult problems.

The location of reference points, materials and equipment stores has similar implications. Display may need to be at adult or child level according to the readership for which it is intended. The teacher's purposes change from time-to-time. Rules for the layout of the classroom are therefore of little value and are no substitute for the teacher's own professional awareness of what is needed.

What is displayed around the school, as well as how it is displayed, has a profound influence on the formation of children's attitudes and values. It is important that art, craft and design work displayed in the classroom and school, other than that produced by the children represents a wide enough range to encourage children's interests in both contemporary society as well as the achievements reflected in the cultural heritage. All local education authorities are now required to formulate a policy on multicultural education and many which have already done so stress the importance of displaying works of art, craft and design from different cultures. Cultural variety is seen as being as much if not more important in the monocultural classroom as it is in schools with children from different ethnic minorities. Some local authorities have accumulated splendid collections of original works and reproductions which can be borrowed for displays in schools and these usually provide information which can be very helpful to the teacher when initiating class discussions. The Commonwealth Institute in London is a valuable source of material illustrating the wide range of art, craft and design of different countries as also are the various Embassies, High Commissions and airline offices.

Having made an assessment of the existing design of the room the new teacher can begin to make plans for change. For the energetic it is sometimes sufficient to ask the question 'I wonder what would happen if . . . ?' There is a difference in what can be attempted in a holiday, before pupils change their classes, from what can be done when classes are already in possession of their rooms. Pupils, particularly younger children, quickly come to depend upon things being much as they were the day before. Changes are noticed immediately and once expectations have been established care should be taken to anticipate the likely response of the class. Frequent minor changes will serve to maintain interest and to sharpen perception, whereas major alterations might be very upsetting.

●FORM AND SPACE

It may be helpful if the teacher adopts a systematic approach in considering the factors which it is possible to change. The teacher may wish to consider how the physical environment of the classroom may be changed or controlled.

- *Are the work surfaces at the best possible height and are they of the most suitable material?*
- *Would it be helpful to cover them with hardboard or polythene?*
- *Could pupils move more easily about the room?*
- *Can obstructions such as cupboards be moved?*
- *Are the larger pieces of furniture, which divide up the spaces, providing the most useful floor areas?*
- *What are the main sources of light and are they free from glare?*
- *Can this be controlled adequately, e.g. with roller blinds or controlled lighting?*
- *Does the room provide for work areas of different character?*
- *Can these be provided in the room or are there better places elsewhere in the school to which children may go for special purposes?*
- *Could such work be suspended from the ceiling?* It might be possible for specialist places to be provided in a school if teachers agree amongst themselves what each would be prepared to provide and for how many children. Practical craft and science facilities are often made available in this way by mutual agreement.

Note: The practicalities involved, for example, in hanging drapes or mobiles from classroom ceilings may be eased with a few kind words to a caretaker. He might be able to offer advice or even practical assistance. However, it is wise not to be over-ambitious and to seek a head teacher's permission before exploring this avenue.

This plan demonstrates how part of a classroom space can be designed as an art, craft and design activities area. It is the result of a working party of Devon primary teachers and is placed here simply to act as a guide for the individual class-teacher.

●COLOUR

Colour is one of the most readily changed factors in the indoor environment. Some colour schemes can be pleasurable and stimulating. Both teachers and pupils can play their parts in selecting and trying out various arrangements of colours. Pupils often say that they do not like this or that colour, but in the presence of varied examples these preconceptions may seem to be very lightly held. The principle of inviting the pupils to participate in choosing is often well to the fore in the reception classes but learning to discriminate is important at all stages of development. This should not be confined to colour but may include all the formal qualities which go to make up objects or events. Teaching children to discern differences is vital to their proper learning of language which is a key issue in the growth of perception.

The classroom provides the enterprising teacher with many opportunities for children to establish a stake in their environment and to discover that their opinions can be shared if they acquire a suitable vocabulary. The discovery that they can help to bring about beneficial change is an important motive for learning.

Scholastic suppliers often supply only crude, sharply distinguished colours and tones. Teachers who seek out more subtle materials find that pupils quickly learn how to describe their preferences. The ability to care about and to make aesthetic judgements cannot thrive where there is no opportunity to exercise discrimination. The alternative is resigned acceptance of what is customarily there. We teachers also find it all too easy to accept with appropriate pleasure or dismay the character of the classroom which is given to us. If the teacher's artistic sensibilities and skills do not enrich the classroom it is unlikely that the children will be encouraged to contribute their own.

Colour comes in a variety of both permanent and temporary materials. The use of coloured material can range from changing the atmosphere of a whole classroom to providing a peephole-experience for one child at a time.

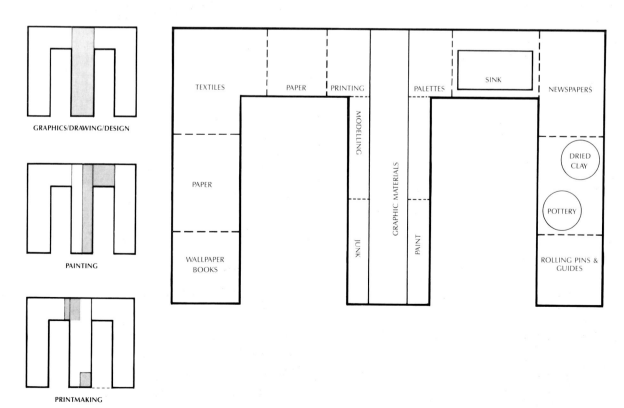

GRAPHICS/DRAWING/DESIGN

PAINTING

PRINTMAKING

TEXTILES   PAPER   PRINTING   PALETTES   SINK   NEWSPAPERS

PAPER

MODELLING

GRAPHIC MATERIALS

DRIED CLAY

WALLPAPER BOOKS

JUNK

PAINT

POTTERY

ROLLING PINS & GUIDES

● OBJECTS AND MATERIALS

Texture is also a factor which can affect the sense of order within a room or can provide a delicate experience which can be sensed only at the fingertips. Touch is an important sense for children as 'handling' and 'grasping' provide means of access to knowledge which cannot be gained in any other way, and classrooms need to provide for all primary school children many opportunities for them to 'know by feel'. Living things, in particular, so long as they are handled with due regard to their needs, give pupils opportunities to exercise tenderness. However, it is in the handling and use of real materials that children make their first explorations into the world of work and technology. All children should handle clay for instance, not only because it is still one of the most widely used and available materials but because its qualities contribute so much to our understanding of language and of ideas like plasticity and fragility.

The ability to hold abstract ideas as images in the mind clearly depends upon having experiences of making images.

It is for this reason that primary classrooms should, from time-to-time, enable all pupils to have access at least to materials for *modelling, shaping, forming, constructing, drawing, painting, printing, weaving, dyeing, measuring*, etc., which give them opportunities to handle and use examples of matter as media.

(Note: A list of materials is given in Chapter 7)

Classrooms must be places where pupils can examine 'real' things. Pupils need to become accustomed to looking at images critically and to enjoying them for what they are. Their drawings, paintings and models, need to be appraised against their own experiences and the experiences of others. This is how the teacher assists in the transmission of our culture, for the pupils' own image-making and their imagination are part of that process.

The well-planned classroom will usually be one in which pupils' work and learning will be much in evidence and where both pupils and teachers share in its maintenance as a place reflecting their mutual interests and purposes. In order to achieve this it might be helpful to:

● set up the classroom as a treasure-house containing both natural and man-made objects which will arouse interest and stimulate worthwhile, confident and enthusiastic activity;

● display things using carefully-considered colour schemes, materials and legible lettering so that the classroom is a pleasant place;

● organise the classroom so that materials, tools and equipment are on hand for children to use as required;

● take a strong, personal interest in what children do so that they can be helped with the relevant skills to do their work well; and

● present children's work through display so that it can be seen, admired, discussed and reflected upon, for display is an extension of the working process.

Well arranged, accessible collections of materials can frequently provide fresh inspiration for creative work while encouraging, by example, a craftsmanlike approach to creative art work. It is essential that from the time children start school they should be taught how materials, tools and pieces of apparatus are stored and how they should be used. This should be an aspect of their education and will cover constructional toys, fir cones for weighing, sand, jigsaws, dressing-up clothes, musical instruments, threads, yarns and materials for creative work.

The class-teacher sets the standards for the careful

use of materials by the way he/she organises the classroom and by his/her personal standards of neatness and orderliness. This is not to say that the book corner will always be immaculate or that the room will not, at times, resemble a jumble sale. At the end of a session or day, however, children must learn to return things to their correct containers or places in the classroom.

The choice of interesting and suitable containers can influence the way in which children carry out these tasks. Discarded cartons or boxes (covered in attractive papers) or cane baskets containing crayons make a big difference to the appearance of a room. They are also usually cheap to acquire. Scissors are easily lost if a careful count is not made or if they are not stored in boxes with a slot for each — which makes counting very easy indeed. Felt-tipped pens will dry out very quickly if their tops are not replaced and so one child might be asked to check these quickly. Brushes will obviously become unsuitable for painting if they are stored standing on their bristles, while unwashed palettes will result in inexact colour-mixing.

A central art materials store to which staff have free access is quite feasible in a school where everyone takes care. Paper should be stored flat in drawers or upon suitable shelves which can, if necessary, be erected using laminated board and building bricks. If materials are locked away then teachers are tempted to have a collection of their own so that they have things available for unexpected occasions, but since few classrooms have good storage facilities, paper can become crumpled or torn, paint is often unused, and many materials are wasted. Just as a teacher needs to maintain organisational rules in a classroom for the benefit of all children in a class, so it is probably good management for one adult to be given charge of a school's central resources and the care of such a stockroom.

It is sometimes wise to look back into a classroom, a unit area, a library corner, the sink area, the store room or the office to see what impression it gives. The environment which we create is often a significant influence on children's attitudes and is an important aspect of the 'hidden' curriculum.

Easy access to materials and equipment will mean that children will need to know where these can be found. If, for instance, a child wishes to represent something in collage materials whilst the rest of the class are using other media, then he/she should be able to go straight to the containers of assorted threads or fabrics.

13. Art, craft & design in a multi-cultural society

Children ought to know something about the diversity and richness of human expression through the visual arts. There is considerable support for the notion that in all our art, craft and design teaching we should take a 'world view' which goes beyond the limitations of any particular ethnic and racial groups in our schools. At the same time, many schools now find that changes in their ethnic balance are a challenge to more traditional ideas as to the nature and implementation of the primary school curriculum. Inner city schools in particular often comprise a number of ethnic groupings, each with its own social, religious and artistic traditions, and teachers in such situations have long seen the need for a broad and flexible aproach to curriculum strategies and teaching methods.

We now have available to us, as never before, music, dance, drama, art, craft and design from many cultures and societies. These are invaluable teaching/learning resources which should not be overlooked as, in the primary school, they provide opportunities for thematic work which allows for a truly contextual approach to specific ideas and processes reflecting the cultural complexity of our society. The aims and objectives of art, craft and design teaching can be realised more fully through a sensitive and informed awareness of the many ways in which different societies and groups have represented their experiences of the world through drawing, painting, pattern-making, costume, the use of colour, modelling, carving and craftwork and through the way they have designed and made everyday objects to reflect and embody their values. Certainly multi-cultural schools have the advantage of

a variety of customs and traditions upon which to draw directly. However, we consider that teaching which stems from and reflects human cultural diversity is vital in all schools and that planned experience of arts and crafts from a wide range of ethnographic origins encourages children to come to terms with objects and ways of life which are unfamiliar, and to learn about the nature of prejudice. We must also be conscious that within *any* culture there are sub-cultures, and the curriculum should take account of this.

Prejudice feeds upon casual perception. It is during primary schooling that children can be taught to take pleasure in observing accurately, identifying similarities and differences in fashion and design and responding with independence and confidence to changes as they occur.

Children at all ages in the primary school have an openness to, as well a fascination for, the images of other, often distant, cultures. Art, craft and design activities should help children to understand:

● the ways different cultures embody and communicate their beliefs in their art, craft and design works;

● that art, craft and design work reflects a variety of sources such as rituals, religions, myths and magic as well as representations from observations and the solving of practical problems;

● that art, craft and design works influence the day to day lives of peoples in different cultures;

● that different rules or criteria need to be considered when comparing and contrasting art, craft and design works from different cultures.

(Extracted from Allison B. (1972) *Art Education and the teaching about the arts of Africa, Asia and Latin America* London: VCOAD)

14. Children with special needs

It is particularly important that children in our classes who may be disadvantaged in some way and who are thus denied certain aspects of the curriculum, should have access to the fullest possible range of artistic activity. Many special schools or special units are provided throughout the country, but it might be helpful to classroom teachers to remind them of the following points:

● Some children might have physical disabilities affecting their work in certain materials normally used in art.

Are there suitable alternatives ?

Could they profit, for example, by using computers while being encouraged to think and work with monitor-based imagery?

- A minority of children like to work on a very small scale in their drawing, painting, modelling or pattern-making. *Could they use small pieces of paper and very fine paint brushes?*
  Is this simply idiosyncratic or does it result from a visual handicap?
- Individuals sometimes fear working alone.
  Are they suffering from a phobia which requires the attention of a specialist?
- Adaptation of work spaces or even brushes may be important.

To be truly creative by imparting personal feeling and endeavour into music, art, movement or words is often the best way of developing self-confidence and self-esteem. It is essential, therefore, that children with special needs are given many opportunities for creative expression and the use of hand-eye-brain co-ordination. However, we need to encourage such children carefully, appreciating what they are capable of doing while recognising that their work may have a special value of its own: a value which may be different from that of other children's work. We must also be careful not to use standard adult expectations to judge unsophisticated forms.

On the other hand, the more familiar we are with the diverse range of art forms which exist the more able we may be to devise appropriate programmes for pupils with special needs.

The atmosphere of a caring community, with all 'types' of children and adults working and learning together is the best stimulation for everyone to move towards his full potential. The child with special needs who is in this kind of classroom will be able to approach artwork with the rest of the class confident that although he cannot, perhaps because of a physical disability, use some tools or equipment in the same way as the others, he can try other approaches or materials. By simple adaptation (i.e. by taping brushes together or fixing water pots so that they cannot be easily be overturned) tools and materials will allow such children access to artistic activities and will help to stop messy work.

Very gifted children may also have special needs. For instance, able children may have a need for more demanding or sustained work. They may require more direct contact with artists (see the section on *The artist and craftsperson in the classroom*) and craftspersons, especially as the work they do may be outside the range of some teachers who, of course should be aware of their inadequacies but who, nevertheless, must give encouragement and support to such children.

This is where the valuable response of an art adviser or a specialist art teacher in a nearby secondary school could be very helpful.

CLASSROOM
PRACTICE

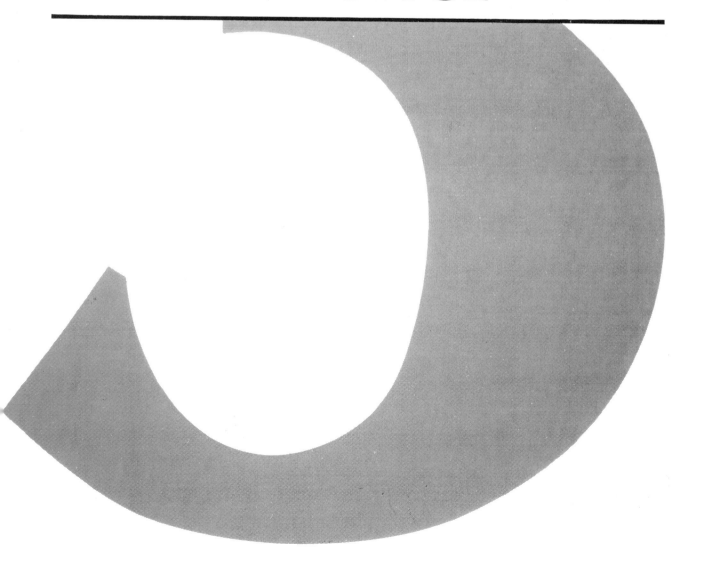

15. Some thoughts about the art, craft and design curriculum

The structure of some areas of knowledge demands a specific and logical pattern of working, whereas art, craft and design education allows for a variety of interpretations and procedures. In spite of this, there is a broad area of agreement about a framework for art education. It is also acknowledged by art educators that however varied the learning strategies may be, they should operate within a recognisable structure. This should provide sequence and continuity, furnishing children with activities which may grow more complex while building upon the experiences already gained.

In order to arrive at a satisfactory teaching strategy, it is necessary to identify the elements of art, craft and design education so that an appropriate balance may be wrought by the individual teacher in the classroom. The following is given as one possible approach which synthesises the ideas of Barrett (1979) and the Schools Council (1978). The work of other writers is also noted so that teachers who wish to read further into the subject may arrive at their own personal solutions.

An approach to curriculum planning in art, craft and design.

The art, craft and design curriculum is concerned with *three* interrelated components: (1) *the child*, (2) *the elements of art, craft and design education*, and (3) *the functions of art, craft and design education*. This inter-relationship is shown in this diagram. Curriculum planning begins with the child. It is therefore crucial for the teacher to have as deep an understanding as possible of the individual child's character, cultural background and environment. As Eisner (1985) put it, 'you start from where the child is'. The majority of art educators agree that art activities encourage the child to build bridges between his/her own inner, egocentric world and the objective world that is outside him/herself, although Gentle (1985) reminds us that art teaching is as much about art as it is about the individual. It is important therefore that we understand the structure of knowledge and experience that underpins the subject.

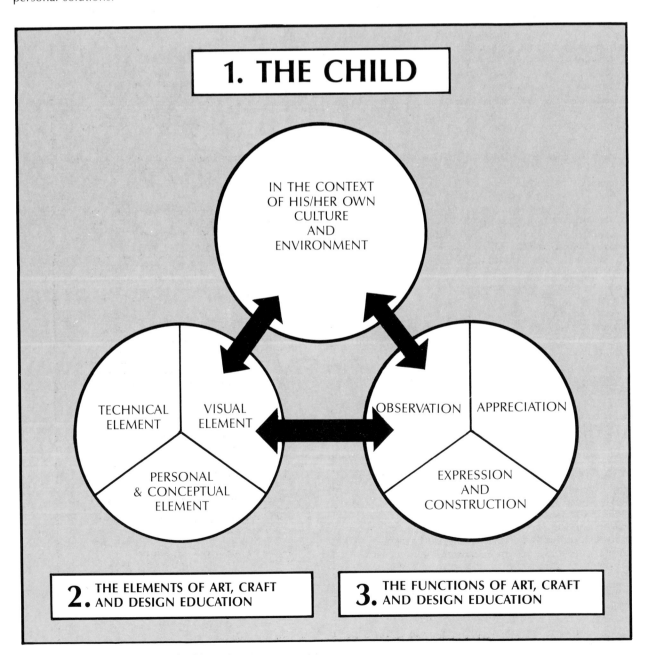

1. THE CHILD

IN THE CONTEXT OF HIS/HER OWN CULTURE AND ENVIRONMENT

TECHNICAL ELEMENT

VISUAL ELEMENT

PERSONAL & CONCEPTUAL ELEMENT

OBSERVATION

APPRECIATION

EXPRESSION AND CONSTRUCTION

2. THE ELEMENTS OF ART, CRAFT AND DESIGN EDUCATION

3. THE FUNCTIONS OF ART, CRAFT AND DESIGN EDUCATION

Barrett (1979) sees art, craft and design education consisting of *three* inter-dependent elements: (1) the personal and conceptual element; (ii) the technical element; and (iii) the visual element.

● *The personal and conceptual* element represents the ideas, feelings or impulses that motivate the creative act. These may already be present in the child or they may be the result of an appropriate stimulus from the teacher.

● *The technical element* is concerned with the materials and techniques which will give form to the idea, impulse or feeling; for example, *paints, pencil, crayon, clay, glue, wood* or *fabric* (materials); *painting, drawing, printing, modelling, sawing* and *collage* (techniques). Attention must be drawn to the fact that children need the opportunity to experience working with a particular technique and material area in some depth, however, if it is to become an effective means of expression.

● *The visual element* deals with the analogy made of the visual world through the use of materials. If, for example, a child draws a flower, he/she may use line, shape, texture and pattern to translate the personal image of the flower into two dimensions. If it is to be a painting then the visual elements involved will be colour, tone and form. In addition to these elements, and bearing in mind the needs of the individual child, there is one more component which must be heeded in this particular approach to curriculum planning and that is an identification of the *functions* of an art, craft and design education.

● In relation to the aims which have been proposed earlier in this book, it must be stated that *the functions of art, craft & design education* are interpreted in widely different ways by various writers. The Schools Council (1978) suggests that the functions of art can be said to include:

- ● recording
- ● analysis
- ● communication
- ● expression

Recording and analysis, it is asserted, are objective activities, while communication and expression are subjective. These activities are not easily differentiated in growing children, but combine in varying degrees.

The main purpose of attempting to identify and describe these functions is to avoid an imbalance in provision. During the 1970s, for instance, primary schools were sometimes accused of putting an over-emphasis on 'free expression', with very little direction from the teacher. In an attempt to redress the balance, some schools are currently concentrating on observational drawing to the apparent exclusion of other aspects of art, craft and design education. **There needs to be a balance between observation and expression in the art curriculum: a partnership between subjectivity and objectivity.**

● One more strand is necessary, however, to complete the balance. *Observation* and *expression* are concerned with the 'making' of art; that is, with the education of the child as an artist, but equally important is the education of the child in the *appreciation* of art. Allison (1973) points out that very few children eventually become artists; *all* become consumers. The activity of appreciation is taken here to mean giving children opportunities to talk about, appraise and reflect upon their work, the work of their peers and the work of others, including the art of museums, galleries and craft workshops.

The functions of art, craft and design include *observation* (looking, recording, analysis), *expression* (communication) and *appreciation*.

Both Barrett (1979) and the Schools Council (1978) suggest that any one of the three *elements* (which is concerned with the three elements of art, craft and design education) may be taken as the starting point for a curriculum development project.

Having presented an approach to curriculum planning in primary art, craft and design which embraces three components — *the child, the elements of visual education* and *the functions of a visual education*, the following two sections will look at possible approaches in the infant school *and* how the individual elements of an art, craft and design education can be used as starting points in arriving at curriculum content in the junior school.

Gentle (1985) identifies four different activities that might be anticipated in curriculum planning:
● exploring, ● ordering & controlling, ● sharing & appreciating, ● inventing & expressing

Southworth (1982) suggests a pattern of art teaching that is sequential and progresses from observation to investigation to communication.

Gentle (1981) says that children's growth is dependent upon external control (ie over materials, objects and movements) and internal control (ie over responses and the capacity to abstract new experiences).

I see the actual work to be done in the art "lesson" as an alternation between the expression of direct, spontaneous feeling with "studies" more objective, deliberately undertaken exercises to explore the possibilities of the medium, to perfect some technique of representation or to become familiar with the workings of nature in a more analytical way. Robertson (1963)

Both participation and appreciation have their places as complementary aspects of arts teaching in cultural education. Gulbenkian Report, *The Arts in Schools* (1982)

Allison (1973) feels that a more appropriate model for art education would be planned for the 'sensitively responding and discriminating consumer'.

Working with children in the area of art necessitates both an understanding of the various developmental stages and a thorough knowledge of the possibilities for growth.
Löwenfeld & Brittain, *Creative and Mental Growth*, 1982 p 33

There is a world that exists beyond the individual world, a world that exists whether or not he exists. There is another world, however, a world that exists only because the individual exists. It is the world of his sensations and feelings. He shares the former world with others. He shares the second world with no-one. Witkin, *The Intelligence of Feeling*, 1974 p 1

Skills & techniques should be seen as a means to an end and not as ends in themselves; however, if they are not acquired, as Best (1979) argues, 'children are . . . deprived of certain possibilities for freedom of expression and individuality'.

It is usually in those classes where one craft — or one group of related materials — is used and developed in depth that craft work of quality and feelings may be found. Schools Council Art 7-11 (1978)

The visual element covers perception and understanding of the visual elements that reveal the appearance of the world . . . Schools Council Art 7-11 (1978)

Southworth (1980) refers to the visual element as "the syntax" of art.

16. Working with INFANTS

Children entering the nursery or infant school handle and look at all kinds of exciting and interesting objects. Collections and displays arouse their curiosity and wonder, and discussions will help them to develop a keener aesthetic awareness and understanding. This, in turn, motivates creative work and becomes a useful source of reference as children *learn how to learn* through looking and touching. The older pupils in the infant school increasingly use close observational studies as starting points for expressive work, and find it helpful if their teachers talk with them about the relationships of visual and tactile qualities, particularly if these relate directly to some of the experiences which they have already had in the classroom or in their own art work, and which will be more meaningful when they look at the work of adult artists, craftspersons or designers. They might examine the bark of trees in the school grounds; attempt to mix colours which are similar to those of stones or leaves; and produce textural qualities with paints and crayons which simulate those of roughly-woven pieces of cloth.

At every stage in their educational development children, including the junior and later the secondary stage, should have opportunities to handle and look at:

- *natural objects—*   pebbles, shells, leaves, plants, flowers, bones, feathers, and so on.
- *man-made objects—*   wheels, boxes, clockwork machinery (the insides of clocks and watches), pots, kitchen crockery, antique objects and ornaments.

They should also consider:

- *inside and outside—*   houses, schools, shops, parks, streets, gardens, woods and fields or the inside and outside forms of shells, peppers or the different textures on the inner and outer surfaces of an orange.

In doing this they will focus on colours, textures, patterns and three-dimensional forms. Above all, as HMI points out (DES 1985), young children will — through *painting, drawing, carving, constructing, modelling* and *designing* — acquire knowledge and skills and develop perceptions which enable them to make a personal response to what they see, touch and feel.

Some of the first-hand experiences might be heightened by the use of *mirrors, magnifying glasses* or *binoculars* to extend the children's vision, while their attention will be drawn to:

- SURFACE TEXTURES —bricks / stones / wood / textiles
- FORM AND SHAPE —stones / flint nodules / bones / pottery / plants / trees / buildings / cars / landscape / pebbles / shells
- PATTERN & CAMOUFLAGE —birds / animals / fish / butterflies / moths / printed textiles / tyres / walls / fences / metal grills
- LINE —drawings / trees / posts / pylons / railway lines / vapour trails
- COLOUR AND TONE—flowers / plants / leaves / textiles / paintings / prints / photographs / dress furnishings / skies / rusty metal

Infant school teachers are generally aware that the provision in each classroom of *a really inviting and lively workspace with its range of carefully-chosen art, craft and design materials and tools*, will often initiate artistic responses by children simply because it is there.

Children delight in experimenting with materials (which will sometimes inspire subject matter) and will express themselves freely through their image-making. In doing so they will also begin to consider the importance of the choice of medium in creating a piece of work (DES 1985). However, the teacher will need to ensure that she provides continuity and progression in the subject through well-considered, sound educational experiences in which pupils can employ designing and making skills. This will be manifested through:

- *simple experimentation with materials* (children discovering for themselves)
- *free-expression* DRAWING/PAINTING/MODELLING and CONSTRUCTING
- *directed experiment* (colour-mixing/textures/patterns in paint/crayon/ink) (form and shape in clay) (depiction of surface images in print)
- *controlled development* (use of discoveries/techniques/skills) in:

DRAWING	—observation/shading/textures (use of natural and man-made forms) (use of plants, animals, humans, fish)
PAINTING	—observation / textures / patterns / colours (use of natural and man-made forms) (use of plants, animals, humans, fish) —imagination (use of stories / events)
MODELLING	—observation / forms / textures —clay and other suitable materials (use of human figures / animals / trees / rocks)
CONSTRUCTING	—observation of buildings / furniture / fences / electricity pylons —constructional kits / boxes / wooden blocks

Topics and aspects could be linked
- Use of developing skills and interests in the production of co-operative paintings (murals), models, costumes, scenery, masks, films *and* individual books, notices and greetings cards or other work depending upon the children's ages and artistic skills.

At this stage it is essential to maintain a balance between child-centred creativity and teacher-controlled activity. Teachers must take a responsible and balanced stance, and by means of thoughtful planning, lead their pupils through soundly-based stages of development. It is therefore vital to achieve a sensible rationale of children's ideas and adult conceptions and this calls for the unique skills and sensitivities which teachers of young children ideally possess.

As children progress through the infant school the teacher will introduce new ideas and stimuli. Displays can be invaluable in developing aesthetic awareness. Materials, new skills and techniques will aid this.

- Providing opportunities for children to handle and explore tools and materials will often lead to rich, creative expression. Through 'play' with paint, clay or paper, for instance, children will learn the properties and possibilties of materials and will begin to acquire control and skills.
- It is important that children make discoveries for themselves, but it is helpful if the teacher takes note of them and, in retrospect, points out the principles involved and how these can be used elsewhere.
- In learning about the properties and possibilities of materials pupils will acquire knowledge and insight which benefits the whole curriculum, particularly if the teacher is aware of what is being learnt and plans to re-inforce this learning. Language, for example, is enriched as such knowledge provides the material for metaphor. Mathematical insights occur as length and breadth are woven together as warp and weft. As pupils discover how to solve problems of construction, how to use levers, how to stiffen a fabric with glue or to allow an adhesive to set, they are exploring elements of technology and design.
- Showing children how to cut or fold neatly, may be the only motivation the teacher needs to give. He/she might comment or pose questions to stimulate thought and action: 'What a lovely hole you have made in this clay. I wonder if anyone lives in there?' Different forms of stimulation may be evoked by the materials he/she supplies.
- Techniques and skills must not be considered as ends in themselves, but rather as a means to developing all manner of art, craft and design work. Collage, for instance, might be used to demonstrate *texture, design, layout, colour* and *pattern-making*; and print-making could be used for *pattern-making, texture, drawing, arrangement* and *colour relationships*. A variety of skills is essential to good craftwork and children should be encouraged to work with accuracy when making things. In doing this they are developing their potential as young designers and craftpersons.
- Primary school children will need to learn skills associated with measuring, cutting, sticking, arranging, poking, pulling, rolling, with materials.

Children's natural curiosity can be capitalised upon in looking at and talking about art, craft and design work whether it is from European or other cultures. The 'why is it like that?' and 'what is it?' questions lead naturally to the 'how do you think other people feel?' questions. The resulting discussions are as important for the development of the imagination as they are for that of language and communication. Children from the infant stage should be developing a verbal vocabulary for describing their visual experiences and learning the particular words which relate to art, craft and design activity, materials, processes and forms.

In addition to offering young children a range of media teachers must also organise the experiences which they provide to take account of the various formal properties that they wish their pupils to come to understand. These can be identified as: *line, shape, colour, tone, pattern, texture, arrangement* and *space and form*. Although such qualities may well be taught incidentally, there is no reason why an active consideration of them should not, at times, be a starting point of art, craft and design activities or a response to the visual aspects of the world, and as a way of developing a visual vocabulary. However, this should not be done at the expense of imaginative work, and a sound way to guard against this happening is to remember that adult artists commonly work by means of a progression from direct observation through to the production of a highly personal response. Teachers might, therefore, develop ways in which children's art education will link the discipline of direct observation with opportunities for them to make imaginative responses. Representational drawing — the process of making images of what is seen — involves imagination and teachers need to look at children's drawings in order to see how the images proposed vary and how all the children represent what is seen. It is important, therefore, that they respond to differences of style observed in children's work and show how they exist in examples of adult art, craft and design.

It is characteristic of successful teaching that pupils are made aware of formal elements to be found in their own work and in the work of others. Pupils need to be helped to recognise differences of style and differences in what each child perceives. This kind of discernment is a basis for developing self-confidence and sound judgements.

The exploration of materials might be an excellent starting-point. Ideas may be suggested in classroom conversations between children and teachers, or they might be stimulated by visits, visitors, "news", stories, films or television programmes. An important factor in motivating creative expression, however, is the use by the teacher of descriptive and stimulating language.

Children must have opportunities to express themselves through *speech, writing, drama, music, dance* as well as *art, craft and design*. Some of these aspects will be closely inter-related and used:

- *to describe daily life & feelings*
  (ie rides in cars, buses, trains & aeroplanes; playground games; shopping, people, pets)
- *to explore ideas about imaginative life and fantasy*
  (ie work based upon imagination, stories, television or drama)
- *to explore the environment*
  (ie handling and looking at objects; comparing visual and tactile qualities, shapes, colours, textures and spatial relationships)

Books or pictures can sometimes inspire art work. These can be useful references which extend general work in art, craft and design but they must be used with discretion so that children do not simply copy from drawings and photographs. They might contain useful illustrations of *fish, animals, birds, people* (their costumes, weapons, homes, transport) for cross-curricular studies or project work. *Architectural reference sources* might lead children to become aware of and begin to understand the shapes, construction, styles and functions of buildings.

Reference materials will vary. In fantasy, for example, consistence is more important than accuracy. The picture story or invention must work in its own 'terms' with little regard for reality. On the other hand, the drawing of a bird's wing leads to an understanding of how feathers are arranged, while a sketch of a pylon will show how it is constructed. Close attention to fact is more important. No fantasy can succeed, however, without some regard to real life and no closely-observed study can be successful without the exercise of some imagination in representation. This is a matter of judgement for both teachers and pupils.

An emphasis is now being placed upon 'designing and making' in art and design education, and an account by a head-teacher of how infant children can *design* (draw/think in two-dimensions), *produce* (construct in three-dimensions) and then *re-look/analyse* (draw what they have made) shows that children can develop through their art, craft and design work a 'real' awareness and expertise as young designers.

AN APPROACH TO 3D ART AND DESIGN-RELATED ACTIVITIES WITH INFANTS

Children live in a real three-dimensional world, and yet many of the tasks required of them in school require the transforming of this world into a two-dimensional representation on paper. Although this has been a fundamental instinct in man ever since the days of cave painting, it is vital that the relationship between the real object and its representation is clearly established, if the process involved in planning and designing is to have a secure foundation. It is a complicated process, however, also embracing the interplay between symbolism and visual match referred to earlier. The process of conceptual development described and analysed by Piaget and others, involves the child in a multiplicity of encounters with the real world upon which he bases his concepts and abstractions about the nature of that world. This process is taken a stage further when the child begins to draw and record his view of the objects in the early years of schooling. Careful encouragement and structured opportunities for the child to observe and draw objects which are around him is one aspect of art education which leads directly into design-related activities, although it must not be seen merely as a preparation for planning and designing. If, alongside such observational drawing, the child is given opportunities to construct and build with a wide variety of materials (brick, junk and commercially produced "kits"), then the two aspects come together. The attitude of adults towards these early model-making activities is crucial: if the models are valued, discussed and treated as an important part of the educational process, increased care and thought will go into their production. A natural corollary of

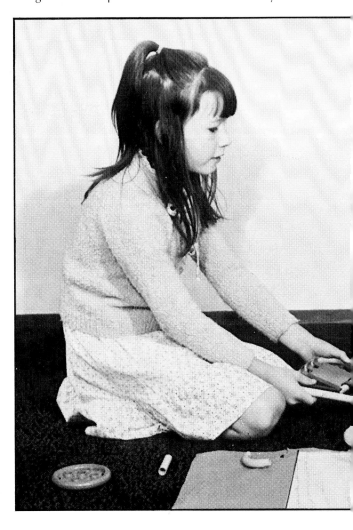

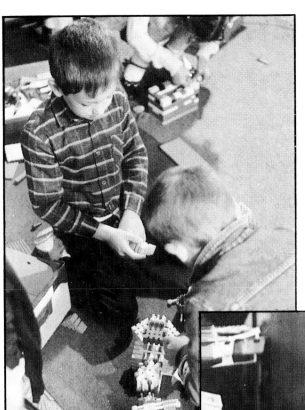

this — given the observational drawing environment described above — is the desire to record the model by drawing/writing.

At the simplest level, this need be no more than "drawing a picture" of what you have made, but with increased familiarity with the materials and expertise in construction a further possibility exists — make a drawing of what you intend to make. This challenge demands a degree of abstract thought, as well as confidence in the possibilities of the materials, if it is to be successful. However, when "design" begins with the construction of the 3D model. The teacher again plays a significant part in developing these design skills and significant questions develop the child's potential (eg. Drawings before *and* after making can be compared — are they the same? Did your drawing tell you all you needed to know? could you make a plan for your friend, so that he could make the same model even if you were not there?, etc.) Such an approach leads naturally into questions of perspective and view ("I can't see all of my model from this side — I need to draw it from the top/side/front"). If these experiences are built into the normal pattern of classroom activity, then children become aware of planning and 'designing' as a natural activity.

17. Working with JUNIORS

The approaches used in working with infants can still form the basis of art, craft and design work with junior pupils and may be developed as part of a continuous process through the primary school. The teaching programme will now become a little more structured and may have stronger links with other subject areas. There will also be an increasing concern for the development of particular skills through art, craft and design activities. The following examples illustrate a number of possible approaches based upon:
1) the personal and conceptual element;
2) the visual elements (eg colour/line etc);
3) the technical element (eg printing/weaving etc); and
4) design and problem-solving

The Personal and Conceptual Element as a Starting Point
A. Example: WHO AM I?

The Visual Elements as a Starting Point
B. Example: COLOUR

This series of lessons is based on the element of 'colour'. Other possibilities would be 'texture', 'pattern', 'line', 'tone', and 'shape'. The Schools Council *Science 5-13 Project* offers ideas which would be particularly relevant in this approach to visual enquiry.

The Technical Element as a Starting Point
C. Example: PRINTING

Here a series of lessons is presented using the technique of printing as a starting point. One school has used this framework for designing a curriculum for every class in the school, and during the year each child spent *one* half term working in the following material areas: *painting, 3D claywork, textiles — weaving, textiles — stitch work, 3D construction work* and *problem-solving*. All areas used *drawing* as the foundation upon which to work. Some art educators hold a contrary view, believing that a technical approach is to be discouraged because techniques are the means (or enablers) only and not ends in themselves.

In addition to the elements identified above design and problem-solving themes may also be used as initial stimuli.
Design and Problem-Solving Themes as Starting Points
Introducing junior pupils to designing and problem-solving in which (i) co-operative themes are employed, (ii) sequentially-conceived developments are planned and (iii) work is displayed, discussed and evaluated, brings them much closer to one approach employed in 'real' life by designers. This necessitates much careful thought — in the planning/design sense; cross-curricular links; co-operative group effort; perhaps the use of 'design briefs'; and the employment of practical skills and techniques acquired previously in art, craft and design activities. Pupils must, however, learn what can be applied to the 'real' adult world.

Here are *two* examples:
D. *Designing & problem solving*
Example 1 *On a theme of containers*
E. *Designing & problem solving*
Example 2 *Structures*

WHO AM I?

ACTIVITY	TECHNIQUES MEDIA & MATERIALS	VISUAL ELEMENTS	ART FUNCTIONS	CURRICULAR LINKS	PURPOSE OF ACTIVITY
① Mark-making with a variety of pencils.	Pencils - as many grades as possible	Line Rhythm Tone	Expression	Language - vocabulary: thin, thick; long, short; straight, curvy; strong, weak etc.	To familiarise children with the properties of the various grades of pencil.
② Self-portraits using mirrors	Pencils - various grades. Children may use more than one grade in their drawing if they wish.	Line Texture Pattern	Recording Analysis Expression	Begin a bio-graphical note book - both visual and verbal: an "IDENTIKIT" - photographs, letters, cuttings, drawings, writing, etc.	To extend knowledge of properties of the pencil. To encourage careful obser-vation.
③ Drawing hands and feet - tensed, relaxed, contorted.	Pencils - variety of grades.	Line Tone Shape	Recording Analysis	Careful written descriptions of hands and feet. A com-parison - what hands do that feet can't etc.	To encourage careful looking. To give further opportunities for using pencils of different grades.
④ A day in my life - drawing time sequen-ces.	Black felt markers	Line Texture Pattern	Communication Expression	Initial drama session to introduce theme. Also a written account of "A day in my life".	To introduce a new medium. I encourage direct mark-making. Also to allow for an ordering of thoughts, first through drama then drawing
⑤ A drawing or painting of you wearing what you have on at the moment.	Choice of coloured drawing materials (pencils, crayons, pastels) OR paint OR mixed media.	Line Texture Pattern Colour Tone Shape	Recording Analysis	Science: children can find out what each garment is made from - experiments with different fabrics. Lang-uage: favourite clothes; clothes you hate wearing etc.	To introduce coloured media. To encourage sensitivity to texture and pattern.
⑥ A drawing of the thing you like playing with best - from observation if possible.	Choice of media - pencils, charcoal, black felt marker, coloured drawing materials.	Line Texture Pattern Colour Tone Shape	Recording Expression	Language: why have you chosen this article in particular? Describe an incident to illustrate your answer.	To provide the opportun-ity for person-al anatomy in the choice of materials to be used.
⑦ Paint a big plate on a patterned cloth. On it paint your favourite meal. Look at some appropriate paintings eg: Matisse, Cezanne	Paints or Mixed media (colour)	Colour Pattern Shape	Communication Expression Appraisal	Language: descriptions of food (Tolkien, H.E. Bates etc.). Science: tasting experiments	To provide further oppor-tunities to use colour and paint. To introduce an apprecia-tion of the work of others.

COLOUR

ACTIVITY	TECHNIQUES MEDIA & MATERIALS	VISUAL ELEMENTS	ART FUNCTIONS	CURRICULAR LINKS	PURPOSE OF ACTIVITY
① Using coloured cellophane on classroom windows - children to talk about their responses when looking out through the different colours.	Red, blue, yellow cellophane	Colour	Expression Communication Appraisal	Language: oral description of feelings evoked by the different colours.	Introduction to colour and its effect on the emotions.
② Children can be given pieces of different colour-ed cellophane and asked to see how many different colour combin-ations can be achieved.	Red, blue, yellow cellophane. May also like to use over-head projector to show advantages of colour.	Colour	Recording Analysis	Science - children may record or chart the colours made. Further work is suggested in Schools Council. Science 5-13 on colour.	Introduction to colour mixing.
③ Choose one of the primary colours and collect objects in this colour for a display (eg: red) Groups of children may like to take it in turns to arrange the displays.	All kinds of visual resources - natural and man made - from palest pink to reddish brown	Colour Texture Form Pattern etc,	Expression Analysis Appraisal	Discussion - children may like to decide how to organ-ise the display eg: warm reds and 'cool' reds or 'dark' reds and 'light' reds or reds you like and reds you don't like.	Developing a more dis-criminating perception of colour - an appreciation of the various tones and shades that exist under the umbrella name of a given colour.
④ EITHER a) draw an irregular grid on your paper (eg: pretend you are draw-ing on a wall) OR b) fold your paper into about 16 compartments Mix reds to match these in the display and fill each compartment.	Cartridge paper paints brushes (of various sizes).	Colour	Analysis Appraisal	Appraisal - discuss the colours that result. What names can you give them eg: tomato ketchup red, bubblegum pink etc, Children might like to make a chart to record how they mixed the colours.	To give experience and confidence in colour mixing To develop colour per-ception.
⑤ make a RED picture EITHER a) from direct observation of some of the things in the display OR b) from imagination eg: The Fiery Furnace The Red Planet The Fire Bird.	Cartridge paper paints brushes (of various sizes)	Colour Shape Form Pattern Texture etc,	Expression Communica-tion Recording	Drama, music and language work stemming from the colour red and all its implications. eg: heat anger danger	To give children the opportunity to use some of the skills they have developed in an expressive way.

PRINTING

ACTIVITY	TECHNIQUES MEDIA & MATERIALS	VISUAL ELEMENTS	ART FUNCTIONS	CURRICULAR LINKS	PURPOSE OF ACTIVITY
① Make rubbings of textured surfaces inside and outside the classroom	Thin paper Wax crayons	Texture Pattern Line	Recording	Use Schools Council Science 5-13 "Textures" to suggest work in science.	To introduce children to the concept of textures.
② Make a textured surface of your own, using the given materials	Card PVA Box of collected materials - string fabric, junk etc.	Texture	Expression	Language development - texture	To extend further experience of texture.
③ Collect textured objects which would provide interesting surfaces for printing.	Found objects eg: cork • polystyrene • fabric Printing ink rollers	Texture Pattern Line	Analysis	The sense of touch - how much greater developed it is in blind people.	To introduce children to the technique of printing.
④ Make an interesting textured surface of your own to use as a printing block.	Line "Pressprint" or Potato (depending on ability of children) Appropriate cutters	Texture Pattern Line	Expression	Implications - Braille. Study of its characters, history and use.	To give children the opportunity to practice making marks on a surface to be printed.
⑤ Look at some examples of prints from a museum or ask your teacher to show you some prints.	Prints from museum loan service - or local comprehensive school or art school (student work).	Texture Pattern Line Shape	Appreciation	Language work - discussion and critical appraisal. Written work of appropriate	To give children the opportunity to see the range of work that can be achieved with print.
⑥ Make a printed design of your own, developing a drawing of some visual resources provided by your teacher.	Lino "Pressprint" or Potato. Appropriate cutters		Recording Analysis Expression		To give children further opportunity to develop the skills necessary for printing.

DESIGN & PROBLEM SOLVING
Example 1 CONTAINERS

ACTIVITY	TECHNIQUES MEDIA & MATERIALS	CURRICULAR LINKS	PURPOSE OF ACTIVITY
① COLLECTION & DISPLAY of natural and man-made containers, inc. shells, 'birds' nests and man-made products of clay, wood, metal, leather, fabric, plastic and paper.	Variety of visual resources — actual objects and photographs.	Drama work to introduce concept of containers and the thing contained.	To arouse design awareness: MATERIALS/ FUNCTION.
② DISCUSSION of a variety of containers with consideration of FUNCTIONAL & DECORATIVE aspects MATERIAL & CONSTRUCTION	Notepaper, pens, pencils discussion & note-taking annoted sketches.	Literature! "Pandora's Box" (or similar). Begin a collection of containers and use as a stimulus to invent own stories.	To develop design awareness: utility decoration technology.
③ ANALYTICAL STUDY of one natural containers (flower head, seed head, nest or shell) and one man-made container (card package hand-bag) to investigate & record constructional details eg. hinges, closures.	Pens, pencils, rulers. Each pupil brings a container - natural & man-made.	Science: use reference books to discover names of seed heads. Similarly shells and the creatures they house. Make a study of different kinds of fastenings in the classroom.	To encourage careful observation & recording & provide opportunity for comparisons to be made.
④ ANALYTICAL STUDY of fabric or paper carrier bag to investigate & record design requirements.	Pens, pencils, rulers. Each pupil brings fabric or paper carrier bag.	Maths: accurate measurement using rulers.	To focus on a design problem leading to construction of design brief.
⑤ DESIGNING own decorative bag in paper or fabric. Ideas/Problems/ Possibilities/Solution.	Pens, pencils, rulers, felt pens, paints, brushes, wax crayons	Survey: make a collection of carrier bags found in the home. Compare designs. Make a graph to indicate class preferences. Find out reasons for preferences. What are the most important factors governing designs?	Problem-solving & design process.
⑥ MAKING decorative bag. Production sequence, tools, skills	White/coloured paper, card, scissors, adhesive.	Survey: investigate the different kinds of bags in use by children in your class.	To develop awareness of relationship between designing & making — ideas & materials
⑦ EVALUATION & TESTING Does it work? Does it look good? How could I improve it?	Discussion display.	Compare with the kinds of bags your teachers use. Are they fulfil different functions? etc.	To consolidate design skills.

The above scheme could be extended to include consideration of containers as environments for animals, birds, fish OR room settings/interior design. Designing/problem-solving could be applied/introduced to other units e.g. PRINTING readily lends itself to presentation of a design brief, such as: 'design a print for a decorative wall tile'. COLOUR could include a design element such as: 'design a brightly-coloured stage set for a play about Autumn & Spring'.

Another scheme of lessons could develop as follows:
● Drawings of facial expressions — FRIGHT, ANGER, CRUELTY, SADNESS, HAPPINESS. ● Stylised drawings/paintings for simple masks — ICE WARRIOR, FIRE GOD, WATER SPIRIT. ● Simple costume design — Adaptation of garments — old shirts, dresses, dress for social occasions. ● HEADGEAR or Footwear. ● Personal adornment — hair styles, make-up, jewellery — PUNKS, TRIBAL DECORATION.

Children will learn a great deal from watching an artist painting on an easel or a craftsperson spinning wool, while an art gallery visit will be made more meaningful if the artist himself is able to talk to them about his work.

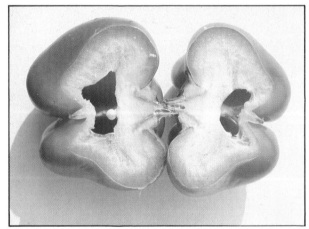

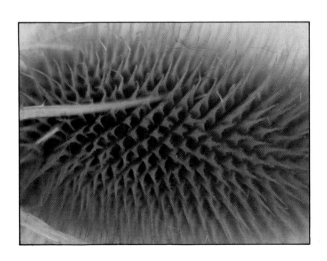

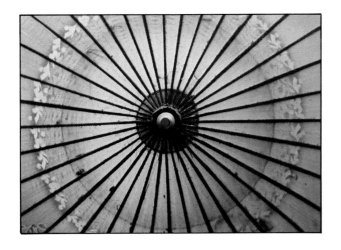

All manner of natural and man-made patterns, forms and textures are to be discovered in the environment. Children can be encouraged to collect objects and pictures so that they will amass useful collections which can then be used as a stimulus for creative activity.

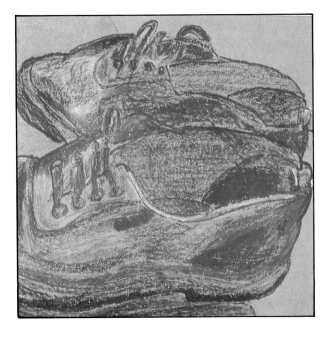

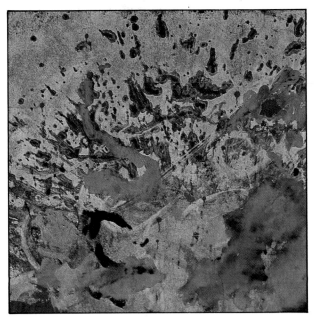

The value of well-considered displays is clear to see in these examples in which teachers have embraced *co-ordinated colours, room corners, simple two and three - dimensional arrangements and ligible headings.*

Drawings and paintings — as seen in these three works by top juniors — can be inspired by *smelly shoes, fishing boats, pit heaps* or many more topics.

When attending in-service art courses teachers will learn a great deal about a variety of art and craft techniques including, as in these two instances, the skills involved in producing prints, and this will give them greater confidence in teaching this aspect of the curricullum.

DESIGN & PROBLEM SOLVING
Example 2 STRUCTURES

ACTIVITY	TECHNIQUES MEDIA & MATERIALS	CURRICULAR LINKS	PURPOSE OF ACTIVITY
① COLLECTION & DISPLAY of natural and man-made STRUCTURES (including photos) spider's web, honeycomb, cow parsley, bridges, electricity pylons, towers.	Collection of various photographs & found objects.	Maths: make measurements and scale-drawings of various structures - investigating the utility of regular solids, beams, arches, etc.	To develop an awareness of various structures in our environment.
② ANALYSIS & DISCUSSION of various structures: STRENGTH, WEIGHT, SPAN, MATERIALS, SECTIONS	Construction of sample structures for testing of strength, weight etc. Weights, rulers, note-books.	P.E: Individual/Partner/group work - investigating body-balance & counter-balance leading to supple apparatus work.	To investigate basic structures, to introduce simple materials technology.
③ Experimental work with card of various sections - strips, folded 'L' section, box profile. Methods of JOINING - lollypop sticks, drinking straws, dowel rods, bamboo canes, card sections, yoghurt cartons, plastic packages, rolled newspaper	Assortment of card, lolli-sticks, drinking straws, canes etc. Selection of adhesives, panel pins, paper clips, brass fasteners, fusewire florists wire	Dance/Drama! Using photographs of structures as starting points to develop descriptive vocabulary for construction. Include voice and percussion for working actions with partners leading to group activity.	To provide for creative use & simple materials & fabrication methods. Introduction of problems.
④ DESIGN & BUILD a model structure bridge or buggy for a stunt scene in a James Bond, Wonderwoman or Action Man movie.	Constructional materials, junior hack-saws, craft knives, cutting surface (hardboard)	History: Historical development of structures such as bridges in wood, iron, stone, steel and concrete.	To provide opportunity to work to a design brief.
⑤ PLAN A SHOOTING SEQUENCE for a scene in a film using the model and Action Man or Cindy Dolls.	Pencils, paper, card, view-finder, stop-watch.	Survey: How many different kinds of structure are there in our school, village, town?	Realization of design solution & three di-mensional planning.
⑥ Shoot the scene using a hired video camera or 35mm slide sequence adding script and sound track.	Video equipment or 35mm camera. Cassette re-corder.	Visit: building/demo-lition sites. What materials have been used? Where do they come from?	To provide first hand experience of media study.

18. Evaluation and assessment

Like all teachers, those in primary education are concerned with *evaluating* their pupils' work, *assessing* their pupils' progress and *education* their pupils to make informed judgements for themselves. It is important that assessment is seen as an integral part of the teaching-learning process.

Whether they are involved with drawing, painting, printing or making models, the work children do is concerned essentially with *successful communication* and the *sharing of ideas*. Before hastening to assess work we need to look carefully at it to understand as far as possible the ideas it contains, while remembering that assessment procedures must reveal pupil progress or lack of it.

The most valuable response which a teacher can make to a pupil will refer to the *content* of the work. *It is not so much a question of what the teacher likes but what the teacher can identify in the work as evidence of the child successfully giving material form to his ideas, which is important.* Teachers do not need to be competent artists or craftspersons themselves to be able to do this, though it helps, but familiarity with the means which artists and designers use will assist them to respond helpfully to what their pupils propose.

Teachers naturally and continuously assess their pupils' work through their talk with them, through their responses to the children's work and through selecting certain work for display. In many schools, the ability of teachers to 'read' and comment upon pupils' work is often sharpened and strengthened through dialogue with colleagues as well as by means of occasional staff sessions in which groups of teachers compare and talk about art, craft and design work from different classes in an attempt to identify what language and assesment methods they have in common when they consider children's work. This kind of sharing can be particularly useful and productive and it can lead to a much better understanding of what kind of work and what quality of response should be expected from different age-groups within a school.

Keeping pupils' work over a period will help teachers to recognise differences in their manner of working, for while it is true that children learn from each other they do develop in different ways. Some, for instance, readily take to making surface patterns, others to the accurate delineation of details; some respond to opportunities to construct in three-dimensional materials, still others make an enthusiastic response to textiles. Recognising these different predispositions can be useful in planning future activity and progression.

It is possible to build-up pupils' success and to establish confidence. Too narrow a concept of artistic ability on the part of teachers can mean that some pupils' abilities fail to receive the encouragement and challenge which they deserve.

The nature and range of tasks we set children within art, craft and design require us to adopt a more flexible system of assessment. Some teachers may feel that we cannot assess by the same criteria tasks as varied as *making a colour chart, drawing a house, modelling a figure in clay, illustrating a poem* or *painting a dream subject*. Others may feel able to identify aesthetic criteria which are not affected by subject matter. We must, therefore, consider this carefully and rationalise our own assessment criteria, making these clear to our colleagues and pupils through discussion.

Part of every school day will be taken up with some form of evaluation of assessment. This is the nature of teaching and it arises in lessons when children ask 'What shall we do next Miss?', or when classes are questioned with regard to their understanding of particular topics, use of materials or application of artistic techniques. Evaluation occurs when teachers ask themselves why things went well, or badly, and when they plan on the directions future art, craft and design lessons should take.

Children's artistic work is so varied and personal that many teachers are reluctant to consider the problem of appraisal in any depth. Evaluation, however, is vital if children are to progress artistically and aesthetically through their primary school art experiences. The central concern of this process is one of *appraising what has happened and what is going on* in order to weigh-up the educative value of the experiences which teachers provide. Because of this evaluation in art, craft and design education must, therefore, be broad in scope.

A marked characteristic of good teaching in artistic subjects is in the way that the teacher sets up with individual children a continuous dialogue about their work as it progresses. The dialogue will consist of exchanges between teacher and child — *some searching, some encouraging, some prodding, some straightforward exchanges of information.*

When children are drawing from observation the exchange is a fairly simple one and will be concerned with ways of making different kinds of marks, ways of measuring, ways of looking carefully. The teacher might say:

- 'Try using the chalk over the charcoal'
- 'Where will you need to use the pencil very lightly?'
- 'Does it really curve as much as that?'
- 'Can you see all of that ear?'

The dialogue will change in emphasis depending upon the task, and so will the balance of assessment that is implicit in this kind of exchange. Dialogue about drawing is mainly about looking — technical matters are supportive to the looking. Dialogue about making a pinch pot in clay is mainly about technical matters. Dialogue about making a drawing of a dream is mainly about notions. Aesthetic considerations will, nevertheless, underlie teacher-pupil discussion.

Although much of what the child has achieved will be evident in the work, there are some perceptions and responses that will contribute to the making of artwork that may not necessarily be evident in its final form. These might include:

- How well the child works co-operatively with other children.
- How much determination is shown in overcoming difficulties.
- How much the child is influenced by the work of other pupils and other artists.

In addition to the informal assessment of the children's work which is part of that kind of dialogue between teacher and child described here, it is important to encourage children towards an appraisal of their own work and that of other artists. The need for this and its place within the art and design curriculum has been appropriately summarised in the recent D.E.S. publication 'The Curriculum from 5 to 16':

> There are two interrelated strands in the development of aesthetic awareness and understanding in schools. One manifests itself through pupils creating their own work, whether pictures, models, plays, mimes or poems: the other comes from experiencing, interpreting or performing the works of other people such as artists, composers, writers or architects. These two strands are mutually enriching and pupils need to interpret what they have heard, seen and felt at the same time as they try to express their own understandings and feelings in suitable media.

They require sources of inspiration and they need to acquire a range of resources and techniques which is gradually extended as pictures are painted, music is composed and played, or plays are devised and acted.

Appraisal has to begin with children talking about their own work. Every art lesson should end with discussion between teacher and the class about what has been attempted and achieved in that lesson. As the children progress through the primary school there should be an increasing use of the work of other artists in support of the children's own work for then children learn a great deal about drawing, designing, painting and modelling through looking at and talking about the work of artists, designers and craftspersons. Just as there is consistent use of the work of writers and poets in support of children's expressive writing there should be a similar use of the work of visual artists in support of children's drawing and painting.

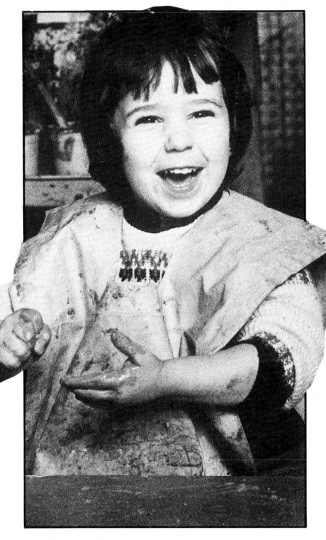

Talking with the children about their work, encouraging them to discuss it with each other, occasionally asking them to write about their work and looking at the work of other artists with them helps teachers in their assessment and appraisal. The following section outlines those different aspects of evaluation of children's work in art, craft and design that need to be considered in order to assess their work effectively. They would prove useful starting points to staff discussion about ways of assessing children's work and towards devising a simple assessment profile of children's progress through the school.

EVALUATION METHODOLOGY
- Comparing of individual children's work in art, craft and design with that of other pupils in the same class. This would include both current and completed work, with the teacher talking with children about it (ie discussions of how individuals have worked and including gentle criticisms.
- Comparing both current work and that done previously. This would involve diagnostic processes which would throw-up strengths and weaknesses while pointing to personal developments and understanding. Teachers might do this through sensitive discussions, questioning and careful observation.
- Making judgements regarding the ability of pupils:
  — to understand and master tasks with specific objectives
  — to acquire problem-solving skills
  — to understand, where appropriate, aesthetic, historical and analytical factors

(1) CHILDREN'S REACTION/MOTIVATION
- *Imaginative, first-hand response to the subject*
  —Originality of ideas, subject matter and materials in developing vision in appropriate ways
- *Pleasure in artistic/creative activities*
  —Enthusiasm and interest
- *Ability to undertake & complete prescribed tasks & self-motivated work*
- *Contributions in discussion & reactions to criticism*
- *Response to individual and groupwork*

(2) PRACTICAL SKILLS (which help to facilitate artistic expression)
- *Mastery of manual skills & processes*
  —Dexterity with subject-related tools & materials (ie paint, crayons, paper, card, wood, clays, rulers, brushes, adhesives and scissors)
  —Confident and understanding use of skills learnt
  —Ability to learn further
- *Appropriate use of skills*

(3) ARTISTIC SKILLS AND PERCEPTION
- *Competence in:* —drawing
  —painting
  —model-making
  —modelling
  —colour-mixing
  —arranging of shapes/forms (ie balance and composition)
- *Sensory and perceptual exploration*
- *Capacity to express ideas & experiences in both 2D and 3D aspects*
- *Sensitivity to the use of colour, pattern, texture and arrangement*
- *Aesthetic understanding and appreciation*

(4) VALUATION SKILLS
- *Ability to appraise artistic and craft work*
  —Use of acquired knowledge to appreciate and value art, design and craft work from past and present cultures in a logical manner
  —Ability to discriminate between techniques, modes of artistic expression as well as between standards of craftsmanship
  —Acquisition of a verbal vocabulary for identifying and describing materials, processes and techniques in a variety of art, craft and design activities.
  —The development of some strategies for describing, analysing, interpreting and evaluating art, craft and design forms.

CHILDREN SHOULD BE ABLE TO MAKE SIGNIFICANT CHOICES FROM A BASIS OF EDUCATED AESTHETIC JUDGEMENTS

RECORD KEEPING is important, for both individuals and groups, within and beyond the school to:
- ensure continuity and direction in the art, craft and design experiences planned both within these aspects and across the curriculum
- monitor individual and group progress and development
- facilitate evaluation of curriculum and lesson content
- facilitate future planning of the curriculum

It will be required for subsequent assessment of syllabuses in art, craft and design.

AN ASSESSMENT PROFILE
In any assessment profile we must be aware of pupil:
(1) *perception* — The exploration and examination of the world through the medium of the senses.
(2) *selection* — The selection of aspects which are perceived and which stimulate us.
(3) *recognition* — The recognition of ideas, feelings and solutions which the stimulus generates.
(4) *expression* — The expression of the recognised response in some appropriate form.
(5) *Materials and Techniques* The development of each child's ability to handle an increasing range of materials with growing confidence and skill.
(6) *Visual Language* The knowledge of and ability to use the basic vocabulary of line, shape, colour, tone, texture, space and pattern from which pictures are made as well as an awareness of the way in which artists in our own and other cultures have used them.

●*PRIMARY ART CHECKLIST*

This checklist is designed to structure our observations of children working. Much of the information can only be obtained through dialogue with the individual child. The simple yes/no response will indicate to teachers areas of concern which the teacher will take action on.

Yes= The child needs no action in this area at this time.

No = The child is encountering difficulties which the teacher needs to investigate further, make decisions about, and take action upon.

● *Sensory explorations*
Does he readily explore his environment through the medium of his senses?
Does his exploring enable him to extract accurate information about his environment?
Does he trust in the information he receives through his senses?
Do his observations result in a more "finely tuned" perception of the qualities which he observes?

● *Selection/Recognition*
a) Does the child have an idea/feeling/response?
b) Do I know clearly what he is trying to say?
c) Is the quality of his idea appropriate to his maturational/intelligence level?
d) *Creativity* The fostering and encouragement of each child's capacity to produce original ideas and solutions to problems which reflect his individual uniqueness.
- Is the idea his own?
  - an amalgamation?
  - an extension?
  - an imitation?
  - a copy?
- Is the idea appropriate to the problem/situation under consideration?

● *Expression*
a) Does his work satisfy him in terms of what he set out to do?
b) Is his means of expression appropriate to what he is trying to do?
c) Has the child chosen his materials with consideration for what they will do?
d) Is the child demonstrating control over the materials he is using?
e) Can he justify his work in terms of what he intended to do?
f) Can he suggest alternative solutions to the problems he is solving?
g) Does he recognize the discoveries and statements he has made?
h) Is he satisfied with his results?
i) Has the work triggered further responses/ideas which he wants to develop?
j) Is the child able to use the correct names to describe materials, techniques and processes?
k) Is the child able to use the correct terms to describe visual properties (including, for example, shapes, colours, lines, tones and textures)?
l) Is the child able to discuss art, craft and design works in a meaningful way?
m) Is the child able to express opinions and preferences for art, craft and design works and give some reasons?
n) Can the child distinguish between art, craft and design works from different cultures?

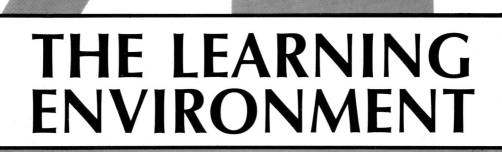

THE LEARNING ENVIRONMENT

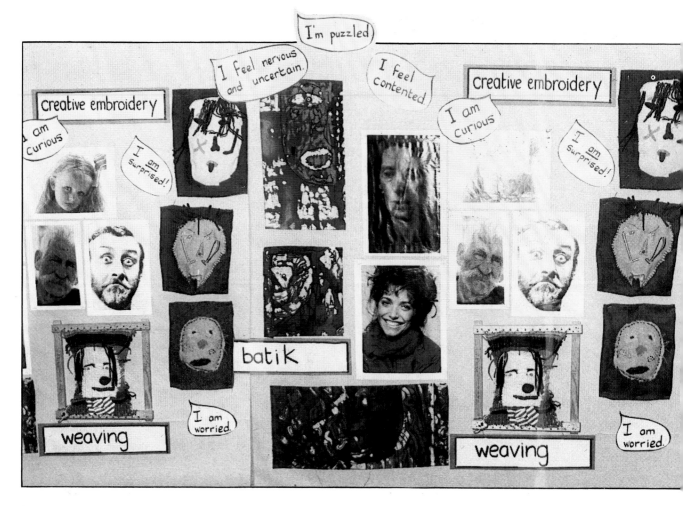

19. THE LEARNING ENVIRONMENT

My own experience of children and students has taught me that concern for display is of great importance in creating stimulating atmospheres. Young children enjoy making collections of natural and man-made objects which they have found and they soon learn how to present these as lively exhibitions in their classrooms; in dark corridors with two or three spotlights introduced to give useful concentrations of light; in school entrance halls where visitors are enraptured by the enthusiasm and expertise of young designers; or in unlikely corners under stairs and in unused cupboards from which the doors have been removed so that these become display units.
(John Lancaster 'The Artist looks at the School Environment', in *Froebel Journal*, 19. 1971, p13).

Aesthetically pleasing surroundings influence both learning and social behaviour. Displays are focal points for learning. They show to a wider audience what children have achieved while reaffirming the value of their work. Displays help children and teachers *to see* things in different ways, and *to make connections* between ideas and materials, different areas of the curriculum, various images, the children's work itself and the work of others — particularly that of artists, craftsmen and designers.

THE PURPOSE OF DISPLAY

Displays should:
1. AROUSE THE CHILDREN'S CURIOSITY;
2. POSE QUESTIONS AND STIMULATE ENQUIRY;
3. FOSTER PARTICIPATION; and
4. SUGGEST AREAS FOR FURTHER EXPLORATION
Well-planned, purposeful displays may be used *throughout a school:*
- as resources for learning across the curriculum
- as a means of imparting information
- to present educational materials well
- as a means of creating visually stimulating learning environments
- as a way of encouraging and praising the efforts which children have made.

CONTENT

Both two and three-dimensional objects and materials may be used in displays, including:
- children's work (paintings, drawings, prints, models, writings, diagrams, maps, charts)
- illustrations, photographs, reproductions, original works of art, craft or other exhibits (LEA Museum and Art Gallery Loan Schemes)
- natural and man-made objects (found objects)
- books, charts, graphs, diagrams and poems
- plants, fish, birds and animals
- information, data, questions, bibliographies/resources
- devices to assist in looking (magnifying glasses, spotlights, microscopes, mirrors and viewfinders)

DESIGN/PLANNING OF DISPLAYS

The achievement of worthwhile effects is brought about by considering the basics of good display.
These might be:

- simple well planned arrangements — often around a 'theme'
- the planning of the layout and consideration of the overall effect before the display is started
- simplicity and no overcrowding
- the avoidance of overlapping, cutting around children's work, the use of pinking shears, the mounting of pictures on a slant, the use of sellotape/drawing pins, garish mounting papers/card/fabrics
- the mounting of drawings/paintings/prints on backgrounds which have the bottom margins wider than those at the top possibly with some material 'window mounted'
- the use (as a general rule) of browns, greys, pale greens, blues and cream rather than brightly-coloured backgrounds
- the use, for backgrounds, of *emulsion paint, hessian, felt, paper, corrugated card* and other suitable materials
- the use of wall boards, screens, panels and display units
- cardboard boxes covered with paper or fabrics, or painted, for use as 'solid' or 'open' stands on or in which to display objects.

It is also important to consider:
- the variety of 2D and 3D objects in any given display
- arrangements, grouping and focal points
- contrasts and similarities
- scale
- children's work and its source material (where appropriate)
- varied heights for 3D objects
- children's eye levels
- lighting (i.e. spotlights)
- simple labels and choice of lettering
- continuity throughout the classroom/school.

The preparation of good displays and exhibitions takes time and effort but the educational pay-off can be enormous. Not only do they give a great deal of satisfaction — making the time spent in producing them worthwhile — but they promote livelier and more exciting learning environments in which both teachers and pupils can give of their best.

Teachers must be prepared, however, and they might find it helpful, to have a basic kit of tools.

DISPLAY KIT

- A Staple gun & lever staple remover
- A Bambi stapler
- A long arm stapler
- Dressmaking pins, & pin pusher
- Double-sided adhesive pads
- Masking tape
- Fishing line
- Panel pins, hooks & eyes
- A tack hammer
- Felt tip & fibre tipped pens for lettering
- A rotary trimmer
- A cutting board & metal ruler
- A Stanley knife
- Scissors including pinking scissors
- A first aid kit
- String & plumb-bob
- Blutak (adhesive putty)

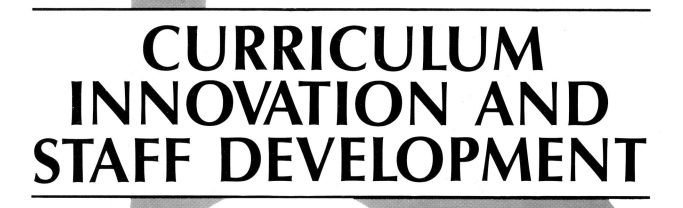

CURRICULUM INNOVATION AND STAFF DEVELOPMENT

20. Support agencies

It is sometimes difficult for primary teachers who are in separate classrooms to think and act objectively in curriculum areas which they did not pursue in their initial teacher training courses. Support is available, however, and the following classification may be helpful:

```
IN-SCHOOL      – head-teachers
   SUPPORT     – individual colleagues
               – curriculum development
                 groups

OUTSIDE SUPPORT  1. LEA advisory services and
                    in-service provision
                 2. teachers' centres
                 3. curriculum development
                    groups
                 4. local arists, craftspersons
                    and designers
                 5. the NSEAD and other
                    professional associations
                 6. LEA art loan services
                 7. art galleries, museums and
                    craft centres
                 8. F.E. and H.E.
                    colleges/polytechnics
                 9. universities
(See opposite page) 10. D.E.S. provision
```

21. In-service provision and L.E.A. adviser support

One of the most important influences on the quality of art, craft and design teaching in primary education is *the type and extent of in-service training available to teachers*. In-service provision for art, craft and design attracts substantial numbers of teachers who are acutely aware of the inadequacies of their initial training. It is often part of the strategy of head-teachers for staff development to link directly specific needs within schools to the professional development of staff. This ensures that curriculum innovation, evaluation and development in a school are much more closely related to the professional development of each member of staff, to the mutual benefit of both teachers and pupils.

Some teachers will find it necessary to plan a structured art, craft and design curriculum for themselves, although this is usually less satisfactory than a coherent 'whole-school' strategy in which the programme is designed and operated as a team activity through school-based in-service work. Team arrangements help to ensure consistency of approach with respect to such matters as specialist vocabulary in relation to the subject, evaluation and assessment of pupil's and teachers' work, and mutual support for all participants.

Where appropriate, leadership for innovative work in the development of an art, craft and design curriculum may be delegated by head-teachers to selected members of staff with special interest, expertise or strong commitments to this subject area. In order that such teachers may function fully and effectively, however, it is essential that procedures be established and resources — including time — be provided for active participation by all members of staff (see the case studies in Chapter 6).

Where there is a complete lack of expertise within a school, or where teachers or the head-teacher feels that it would be more advantageous to involve outside sources of reference, it will be necessary for them to select from various support agencies providing assistance. In enlisting the help of an 'outsider' it must be recognised that the planning of an art, craft and design curriculum is not a 'one-off' exercise for it will need to be adapted to changing circumstances within and beyond the school. Neither can their planning be done in isolation from the rest of the school curriculum and an outside specialist consultant would take account of this.

The role played by outsiders in supporting the development of art, craft and design will depend largely upon the location of a school and its proximity to sources of advice and support. Some LEAs have art advisers as well as advisers for primary education, and several have produced excellent *guidelines* for the teaching of this subject at primary level. These provide the basis for the structuring of well-balanced programmes of study and ensure that advice is available from experienced specialists.

Art advisers usually arrange appropriate in-service provision enabling teachers to implement suitable schemes of work. Occasionally they will arrange for teachers to visit other schools where good practice exists, and they will help to promote confidence and an understanding of this curriculum area. Advisers will, from time-to-time, arrange exhibitions of primary work in art, craft and design which can be very helpful to schools in planning and evaluating their own programmes. The opening of such exhibitions — which may be attended by school governors, local politicians, parents and primary and secondary school teachers — can be a strongly motivating force for further curriculum development. However, initiatives of this kind require a great deal of thoughtful planning and the quality and commitment of the in-service course tutor will be a decisive factor in promoting such developments.

Some LEAS are unfortunate in that they do not have specialist art advisers and are therefore obliged to seek guidance elsewhere. However, many primary advisers have considerable expertise in offering assitance and organising in-service workshops. This may be available at teachers' centres — bearing in mind that the provision of this kind of support varies considerably between different local authorities — and where a teachers' centre is accessible to a school the head of the centre will usually be prepared to help, especially if the head-teacher is able to give specific details about the school's requirements. Heads of teachers' centres usually have networks of contacts to refer to for specialist areas of the curriculum, and are able to negotiate consultancies fairly quickly to provide appropriate expertise. More usually, however, at least a term's notice will be needed to arrange special programmes of support, for most in-service work is planned and budgeted for at least one term in advance.

OBSERVATIONS MADE BY THE HEAD OF A TEACHERS' CENTRE

- The 'tips for teachers' course is of limited value, although it is arguable that for many teachers it may provide a first toe-hold for them to learn about art, craft and design education. This kind of provision, however, must be seen in the context of the present standard of art education in certain primary schools. While there are schools in which the subject flourishes and makes a unique and outstanding contribution to the pupils' education, there are also schools where this is not the case. In such circumstances, even the prescriptive, solution-centred type of in-service provision will, to a certain extent, improve upon what is being taught at present.

HELP! from OUTSIDE the school

WHO?

- HMIs (DES provision)

- Art advisers
  Primary advisers
  Advisory teachers
  (LEA provision)

- Teachers'Centre leaders

- Universities
  Polytechnics
  Colleges of FE & HE

- Art & Craft centres

- Galleries
  Museums
  Education officers

- NSEAD

- Local artists, designers & craftpersons

- Curriculum Development Study Groups

HOW?

- organising award-bearing courses

- organising non-award-bearing courses

- initiating school-based in-service courses

- initiating teachers' centre in-service courses

- setting-up working parties

- promoting study groups

- establishing liaison groups between primary and secondary schools

- planning study-visits

- lectures

HELP! from WITHIN the school

- Head-teachers

- PSRs (teachers with posts of special responsibility for art, craft & design)

- Individual colleagues

- Curriculum Development Groups

- Teachers, NNEB or ancillary helpers with expertise and interest in the subject

- encouragement and interest

- initiating school-focussed, school-based in-service work

- team teaching

- example — ie use of displays and exhibitions

- Many primary school teachers are acutely aware of their lack of expertise in what, to them, is a vital curriculum area and are anxious to do something to improve their situation. This is why most INSET courses in primary art and craft are over-subscribed and are usually very successful in outcome. It is apparent that given appropriate in-service opportunities and effective follow-up support in schools, many primary teachers will often go to considerable lengths to improve their teaching.
- In my experience, the best kind of in-service provision for art, craft and design carefully balances *theory* and *practical work*. Teachers need to explore WHAT they can do in practical terms, as well as having the opportunity to discuss the *VALUE* of activities in educational terms and WHY they are doing it. This introductory phase may need to be fairly rudimentary if participating teachers have had little experience in organising art and craft lessons. It is often surprising to find how little some teachers think they know about materials and techniques, in which case the first priority is to pass on basic knowledge and encourage confidence. Having established this in the early stages of in-service work, teachers can then be offered guidance in structuring programmes of work around an appropriate curriculum framework. If this is done effectively, most of the fears about an over-prescriptive approach can be allayed. Many primary teachers are keen to develop their own programme when provided with appropriate guidelines and professional support.
- Even the best In-service provision cannot be really effective in improving the quality of teaching unless there are adequate opportunities for 'follow-up' within the school The primary school head-teacher plays a crucial role in this (1) by organising staff meetings and discussions to evaluate new ideas (2) by suggesting ways in which these may be introduced in the different classes throughout the school, and (3) by allocating an adequate proportion of the school capitation allowance for the purchase of materials and equipment.
- It is often a good practice when organising in-service provision in art, craft and design to invite participating teachers to arrange exhibitions of their pupils' work a term or so after a course has finished. As well as placing responsibility on participants to implement and develop the ideas gained on the courses, they offer meaningful contexts in which longer-term evaluation can be conducted and provide useful evidence of how original in-service material has been adopted or adapted to accommodate the needs of different groups of pupils.

(Supporting material in the form of *An Infant School Case-Study* and *An In-Service Case-Study* will be found in Chapter 6).

22. The National Society for Education in Art and Design

Further support agencies such as local groups of primary teachers, art teachers, art centres, and the like, may be available to both individuals and to schools seeking to initiate and sustain artistic/aesthetic development. Foremost amongst these is the NATIONAL SOCIETY FOR EDUCATION IN ART AND DESIGN (NSEAD) which operates on a district basis throughout the country. Its membership is drawn from a broad spectrum of interests in art, craft, design, art education and art history, and includes college lecturers, art advisers, administrators, as well as primary and secondary teachers. The NSEAD exists to promote art, craft and design education and is eager to support staff and curriculum developments across this curriculum area. A notable example of the kind of support given is the annual award of the NSEAD/BEROL BURSARY for teachers who wish to invetigate the possibilities of innovative work in art, craft and design. Meetings and courses are organised by local NSEAD groups and non-members are encouraged to attend. Informal contacts made in such meetings can often provide ideal opportunities for discussing day-to-day problems with professional colleagues.

CONTACT with local groups can be arranged by writing or telephoning the General Secretary, NSEAD, Head Office, 7A High Street, Corsham, Wiltshire SN13 0ES.

This office also holds the addresses of other associations such as the *Crafts Council* the *Arts Council*, the *Design Council* and a number of *Regional Art Societies*.

23. Art galleries and museums

Advice and support can come from other sources, too, and there is an increasing tendency for art galleries and museums to offer such assistance. They will, through their educational support services, collaborate with schools in programmes of work concerned with art education and teachers should find the following comments by an art gallery education officer of interest:

- Galleries represent 'local' resources. As far as the primary teacher is concerned, they may provide the services of an 'independent' professional art teacher; exhibitions and/or permanent displays of art; exhibiting and/or local artists; books, catalogues and postcards. Some galleries are happy to provide materials for school use in the galleries or in the study room; some may provide relevant slides for the purposes of preliminary work for a visit; others will lend exhibits to schools.
- The *first* of these resources, however, must be exhibited work itself. This is the resource which dictates the approach of the gallery art teacher (or where funds are insufficient for a trained teacher, the gallery assistant), and ensures that whatever project entered into with the gallery will necessarily involve an exchange of different objectives. This is important and fundamentally useful for children grow through being exposed to mature work and through working with artists who devote their lives to the practice of art. Children also benefit from working with people who have different expectations, different methods of reaching them and generally an openness of purpose which suits the 'additional' nature of gallery projects in relation to the school curriculum.
- Teachers will need to plan visits carefully and it is wise to do this in conjunction with gallery or museum staff well in advance.

Clearly the message is that resources and professional expertise are there for teachers to use (see the example of an art gallery project).

It must be stressed that the use of situations away from school adds an invigorating excitement to children's learning experiences which, though difficult to quantify, is invaluable. Children see such experiences as being different from normal school work and they certainly give a tremendously important stimulus to both individual and co-operative curricular activities.

24. University, polytechnic and college support

Both award-bearing and non-award-bearing courses concerned with art, craft and design are available at many institutions across the country Some colleges also mount in-service programmes, lectures and conferences for teachers. Lecturing staff involved in such work are often prepared to act as specialist consultants and to arrange appropriate support for school-based curriculum development work and school-focused study groups (see 'A one-day in-service course', in Chapter 6).

DETAILS OF COURSES are available in college prospectuses but information about other services provided by specialist staff is best obtained through direct contact with individual colleges.

Such work is often complemented by Her Majesty's Inspectors of Schools (HMIs) who arrange programmes of in-service courses and conferences for primary teachers.

25. The artist and craftsperson in the classroom

One of the most stimulating ways of encouraging interest and involvement in creative activity is for a school to invite artists and/or craftspersons to work alongside children. Spare classrooms can be turned into temporary studio/workshops or, if no such classrooms exist, the guests can be encouraged to use a corner of a classroom or the school hall. Some highly qualified artists/craftspersons are only too delighted to pursue their skills in close proximity to young children so that both pupils and artists work alongside each other. *This will enable young children to experience art, design or craftwork being made by professionals often for the first time in their lives.*

Colleges of art, technical colleges, polytechnic faculties, institutes of higher education or sixth-form colleges are often prepared to help, and young art and design students are usually quite pleased to have opportunities to spend a few days or, in some instances, even a complete term working as 'artists/craftpersons in residence'. Schools might:

- approach a local college or your LEA art adviser for guidance on this matter
- education officers of the Arts Council and Crafts Council of Great Britain
- seek the help of a regional art association
- invite local craftspersons into school

When an artist, designer or craftsperson is in a school it is interesting to observe the children:

- watching what is happening very keenly;
- asking questions;
- involving themselves in conversation with the guest;
- learning new skills; and
- developing a keener sense of wonder and appreciation of the work of others.

They are excited by having a creative person working in their school and the spin-off into other learning situations is interesting. This is seen as a real-life activity for children are then very much involved. The use of such a scheme should be considered. The advantages are great both for the pupils and the school, and they can be most helpful to the classroom teacher. Experiences of this kind can give young people first-hand evidence of how artists and designers work an how they gain satisfaction from meeting the demands of their crafts.

26. LEA art loans services

Some LEAs have their own Art Loans Services as an educational support agency for schools and colleges. These may be under the control of an experienced art teacher or a museum/gallery-trained person, and will augment the resources available in local art galleries and museums.

Schools' Art Loans Services will probably contain a range of art, craft and design work by professionals — including sculptures, textiles, paintings, prints, films, slides, furniture, pottery, calligraphy, cutlery and a range of materials concerned with interior design or fashion — which can be booked for loan to a school.

27. HMI support for teachers

Within the total education service Her Majesty's Inspectors constitute a comparatively small body which is responsible to the Secretary of State for Education and Science for inspecting all education establishments. Some 500 work throughout England and Wales. Of these approximately 20 share responsibility for the inspection of art and design in all schools and in colleges of further and higher education. Like other subject specialists they are deployed throughout the regions and undertake general as well as specialist responsibilities. Every school has a designated HMI as its general inspector who acts as a point of contact with HM Inspectorate and the DES.

Because of their special opportunities to become familiar at first hand with many aspects of the education service, HMI are often able to offer advice and to draw attention to trends and developments of which they become aware in their travels.

Close inspection of work in progress is the only sure basis for accurate reporting to the Secretary of State on the quality of the education service. The publication of these reports, which do not comment on individual teachers, enables others who have responsibility for aspects of the system and members of the public to have the benefit of an independent commentary. In addition to inspection reports, more general reviews are published from time-to-time to encourage discussion of curricular issues and changing expectations or circumstances in schools. Descriptions of good practice in art, craft and design have provided useful guidance for teachers. Details

are noted in the bibliography.

More directly HMI are glad to share with teachers their observations on more particularly professional matters arising from their inspections. Opportunities for this occur in art and design when specialist HMI visit schools. Although brief such discussions are often valuable because they occur where the work is being done. The circumstances in which we work in art and design are very variable and are an important influence on what we do. HMI value the opportunity to also contribute to local authority courses and teachers groups when invited though they often work away from their base for quite long periods and may need advanced notice and alternative dates.

Some courses are arranged with DES support on a regional basis. These draw together teachers from a wider area, usually from more than one authority and deal with issues or topics of general interest. They often lead to school-based research by teachers which is fed back for the benefit of the study group. Any institution, individual or group can propose such a course. DES funds are available though naturally limited. Each region has a committee which examines proposals and recommends priorities for funding. HMI can be consulted at an early stage by anyone who identifies a need which might be met by a regional course. Examples of recently approved and funded courses in the art and design field include studies in the history of art for art teachers, ceramics in school and computers in aesthetic education.

Most teachers are familiar with the booklet headed "HMI SHORT COURSES FOR TEACHERS" which is published by the DES each autumn. This gives details of courses planned for the following financial year. It is supplemented by posters and blue-headed leaflets giving details of individual courses. Application forms for DES courses are held by local education offices to which they should normally be returned when completed by the teacher. These national courses deal with issues and topics which are of national and sometimes international importance. In addition to their content most teachers find these courses to be of value because of the opportunity they provide to meet colleagues with similar professional interests who work in different circumstances in other parts of the country or abroad. A sense of participation in a very large enterprise is often supportive and beneficial.

HMI occasionally publish reports concerned with aspects of art, craft and design education which can provide useful guidance to the classroom teacher.

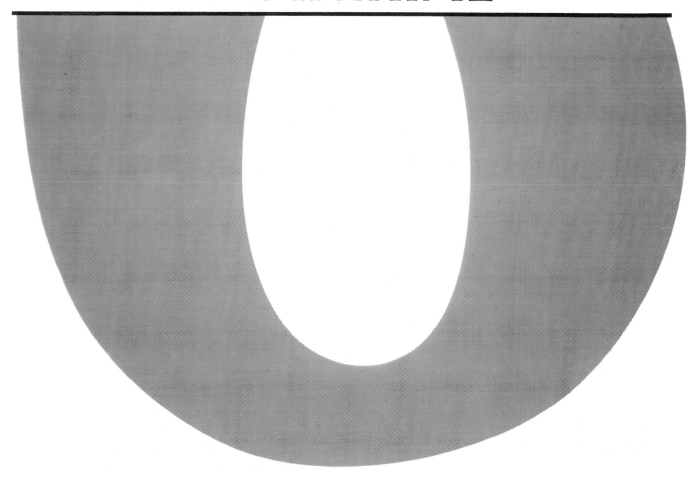

SUPPLEMENTARY MATERIAL

28. A one-day in-service course

This is a brief description of a typical, one-day course for teachers which was organised and taught by a tutor in a local teacher education institution. It was put on for the staff of one infant school, all of whom attended, and aimed quite simply (i) to examine starting points from direct experience, (ii) to consider appropriate media, methods and developments for expressive art work, and (iii) to show how such an approach can be used with children.

The course opened with a short discussion about different ways of stimulating expressive work and this led quite naturally into a consideration of suitable media and techniques. Using a collection of stuffed birds as a starting point for practical work, each teacher selected an aspect for development which involved media which she had not used before. These included the *analysis and matching of colours by mixing paint: the examination of soft textures and feathers using oil pastels; the use of fabric collage to depict pattern, shape and surface textures and colours;* and *mark-making with assorted tools.* Towards the end of the session the teachers began to consider ways of developing these experiences with children, together with the use of expressive language.

Teachers returned to the afternoon session with a group of three children from her own class whose academic and practical abilities varied. The college tutor developed a discussion about the birds with the children while the teachers set-up a workspace and organised materials. Each teacher then organised a practical session with her own small group, which enabled her to look closely at and to discuss ways of working with the children. The children were questioned as to appropriate colours for beaks, wing feathers, the birds' legs; they discussed how legs and wings were joined to bodies; and they attempted to cut paper and fabric shapes which were like feathers The session concluded with everyone looking at the work which the children had produced. This was discussed and the course itself was given a brief evaluation.

The fact that the school had closed for the day had enabled the teachers from it to work together as one group, and allowed them to discuss together the development of art work throughout the school. They welcomed the opportunity to try fresh ideas and media and to explore these with the children. Everyone agreed that they gained confidence through the experience. Although the course could have been held on the school premises it was felt that a change of environment was valuable. These teachers were also stimulated by the work in the college's art department and said that they better appreciated the role of the college as a resource.

29. An infant school case-study

The staff of an infant school was concerned about the level of art and craft-work being done with the children and so a specialist tutor from a local teacher-education college was invited to visit the school to discuss this with them.

Several teachers felt insecure about their own abilities in art and most needed fresh ideas about what to teach their pupils. Five short evening sessions were arranged in the school (starting at 4.00 pm) and these were concerned with *stimulation, development of work* and *display and presentation* and to *the formation of some art and craft guidelines* for the school. They also gave an opportunity for teachers to use new media and skills. After each session the teachers were encouraged to try out the work with the children and bring it to future sessions for discussion and evaluation.

● *Session 1*

The session started with a discussion about the role of art in school and the ways it is used is as a subject in its own right; integrated with other subjects such as drama, music and language; part of topic work; and how skills gained through art activities aid learning in other subject areas. Slides of children's work were shown to extend discussion points and ways of stimulating creative activity were considered. A wide range of media was available and a variety of objects such as *stuffed birds, shells* and *pieces of machinery* were provided. The teachers were encouraged to select one object which would act as a stimulus for a short art programme in which children would expand ideas of *colour, pattern, form* and *texture.* Appropriate media or skills which would develop the theme further were discussed and the teachers explored the practical possibilities in a workshop session. Discussion was based on the aims and objectives the teachers set for themselves.

● *Session 2*

The work done by the children was looked at and compared with the work done by the teachers in the previous session. The teachers then worked together in pairs to consider ways of developing the themes and they planned two or three lessons based on their starting points.

Fresh ideas for use of media and some new skills were introduced and the teachers explored their ideas through a practical workshop.

● *Session 3*

Small displays of the work done by both teachers and children were mounted. The emphasis was on showing what the themes were about and how they were being interpreted and developed, but some help and advice was also given on the arrangement and appearance of the displays. The displays were mounted in the hall to enable the whole school to see and discuss the work.

● *Sessions 4 & 5*

After an initial discussion the teachers split into groups to consider the project and how, for instance, a theme such as 'colour' could be developed throughout the four years in the school, and the different approaches needed to enable development to take place.

The tutor provided some sequenced guidelines for art and craft as a basis for further discussion, and groups were asked to draw-up lists of art and craft skills, activities and experiences they would expect to provide for children at different stages in school. The lists were analysed and formed the starting point for an art and craft syllabus for the school.

● For the rest of the term the tutor visited the school to give help and advise with the planning and the development of the syllabus and each teacher took a section of the work to be developed with the children for the following term, while visits were made to individual members of staff to give advice and practical help.

● The following term the tutor spent one morning each week in the school, giving practical help to teachers where this was needed and working with groups of children to enable teachers to see ideas in practice. Confidence quickly developed and a stimulating atmosphere was built-up, with teachers giving help to each other as a team. Several displays

of work were mounted to enable teachers to see what everyone else was doing, and topics were quite varied. These included: 'looking at spirals', 'inside and outside,' 'looking at faces', 'happiness' and 'sadness'. The participants felt that this project was a success and that further projects could be developed from it.

30. An in-service primary school case-study

What follows is an account of an in-service course in primary art and design education held at a teacher's centre.

● (1) *The design of the course*

It was intended to provide opportunities to work with materials and to extend understanding of art education. The course aimed to help teachers *to appreciate art as an effective tool for learning* which is at the very centre of the curriculum.

● (2) *The content of the course*

The *eight* sessions which constituted the course included a balance of discussion groups, curriculum development groups, formal lectures and practical workshops.

Session 1. Discussion: 'The purpose of art and design education and its place in the school and society'. Course members' views were elicited first, followed by a formal lecture and further discussion.

Session 2. Lecture and Discussion: 'Curriculum design in primary art education'.

Practical session: 'The importance of assessment and evaluation in curriculum design'. The drawings of an entire class of nine-year-olds were pinned up on the wall and course members were asked to place the drawings in rank order, without conferring with their colleagues.

The results were discussed and implications considered.

● *Session 3. Slide presentation:* 'Curriculum design in practice'. This showed a scheme of work in drawing, painting and printing which had been developed with top juniors over the period of a school year.

● *Sessions 4, 5 and 6. Three practical workshop sessions* in which teachers were asked to play the role of children being taught part of the scheme of work presented in session 3.

The three practical sessions dealt individually with *drawing, painting* and *printing*. Course members responded at their own levels of ability in art.

● *Session 7. Practical session:* 'Curriculum development'. Course members working in groups of 4 or 5 were asked to design a sequence of three lessons in drawing. They were advised to consider the following points:

● the age of the children to be taught
● the materials and techniques to be used
● objectives or principles of procedure or the sequence
● how it might be evaluated and assessed
● how the work might be extended further both in the art activity and in other curriculum areas.

Each group was then asked to present its programme to the others and comments were invited. Some members tried out their sequence in schools and reported back in the following session.

This proved to be a most stimulating exercise for all concerned.

● *Session 8. Course evaluation:* Groups were given the following questions to discuss:

● Why did you enrol for the course?
● Was it what you expected? (What did you expect?)
● What did you like/dislike about it?
● How might it be improved?
● What would you like further courses to include?

A plenary discussion was held in which the responses to questions were correlated. Based on the information gathered, some conclusions were drawn and a report written. This was shown to the teachers' centre warden, who had copies made which were circulated to the Chief Adviser and the head-teachers of the schools concerned.

● *Summary of the teachers' evaluation of the course*
Teachers appreciated the balance of theory and practical experiences and the opportunity for personal exploration in the various techniques (drawing, painting and printing). They found the session on evaluation and assessment of particular benefit. It was felt that the group discussions had been stimulating and valuable in helping to clarify their own thoughts and through hearing the views of colleagues.

Some course members believed that there should be separate courses for infant teachers and junior teachers, whereas others welcomed the opportunity to hear the views of those teaching different age groups.

Members felt they needed further courses to extend their knowledge in certain specific areas of art education, i.e. in painting and colour, in three-dimensional work, in textiles and also in evaluation and assessment procedures.

● *Conclusion*
The course aimed to increase the teachers' confidence, and also to use their expertise as fully as possible. They already possessed much of the knowledge and experience necessary for designing curriculum projects in art and design, and the seventh session of the course provided an opportunity to make this apparent. There is no substitute for experience in the classroom and the good primary school teacher should never be allowed to underestimate his/her contribution to the education of the child. It is up to head-teachers and advisers to ensure that teachers recognise the importance of professional development and the relationship of this to the curricular needs of the school.

THE NSEAD BELIEVES THOSE WHO DEAL DIRECTLY WITH CHILDREN IN THE CLASSROOM HAVE A SPECIAL RESPONSIBILITY TO INFLUENCE THE COURSE OF ART, CRAFT AND DESIGN EDUCATION IN FUTURE YEARS.

31. An art gallery project

Through *one* gallery project undertaken by the education staff in a large provincial art gallery, entitled 'GALLERY AND SCHOOL, ART STUDY COLLABORATIVE PROGRAMMES', considerable progress was made in terms of the children's own visual language as well as their assessment of their own capabilities. The school was a local LEA junior school with a strong racial and cultural mix. The group of children involved was brought together on 'a withdrawal basis' for extra help in Maths and English, and their ages ranged from 8 to 10 years. The project sought to encourage the children to extend their own visual language through an investigation of colour. 'COLOUR AS LANGUAGE,' we called it, and 'we' were myself as gallery based teacher, the school teacher (Maths trained!) and a local artist. The project was based on direct

day, and showed slides of artists' work where colour had been used expressively. The *third session* was spent filling in a plan of the school with colours appropriate to how we felt about that particular part of the building. Practical colour exercises and investigations were therefore quite specific; and directed-observation, expressive exercises and discussion preceded the first visit to a gallery.

● The *first visit* to the local municipal art gallery directed the children to see very carefully-selected work by artists such as *Matthew Smith, Pissarro,* and *Courbet and an uncharacterstic Seurat* (a very early Sunset). Pupils were given the chance to select one of ten paintings, each one indicating a particular mood which represented a time of day or a particular season. Paper and water-based pastels were then used to work from the selected

observational studies and was under-pinned by a rigorous approach to an understanding of colour, the colour palette, colour mixing, colour harmonies, discords, hues and tints — all beautifully set out in the school's own communal art guidelines and syllabus.

Each observational session was carefully prepared for by new research into what colour — and mark-making with colour — can do. The *first session* took place in the school field, with the children making paintings of a selected area; the *second* was in school, and was devoted to tightening up on the initial reponse by stretching the children to mix and use colours to make an *exact* representation of the kind of day and time of year. We discussed colour as a way of expressing mood, the feel of a particular

image. No child hesitated and no-one talked or rushed around, even though several of the children are disturbed in their general behaviour. None were overwhelmed by the strangeness of the gallery because they had an interesting job to do. They simply got on with the task in hand *because* it was part of a carefully constructed programme of art study and the visit represented no more or less than the next logical stage.

● The balance of practical and theoretical sessions was repeated as a preparation for the *second* gallery visit when the children could see a large exhibition of colourful abstract paintings by William Henderson on 'mark marking' (the thinnest line, the thickest, the tightest circle, etc). They also responded to the sense of words like "slam" or "cold". Sessions on responding to sounds in rhythmical pattern were all undertaken in preparation for the visits.

Again the "event" of the first visit was minimised as the children immediately started to work with a peephole view of a selected painting by Bill Henderson. Bill was there to chat to the children about his work and about that of the children. At the end of the day he criticised the work as a whole and hinted at approaches to be avoided. The children loved talking to him (were not so keen on him talking to them) and showed not the slightest hesitation about working with paintings.

- The *third* visit gave each child the chance to work from a whole painting, perhaps 10×8 feet, and again this seemed to fire their enthusiasm and encourage them to work very specifically in their

stimulate children with learning difficulties and who often don't like being at school.

Comment

Is this different from any other school project? In some ways, quite obviously not. In the use of practically-based gallery visits; in the preparations guided by art practice normally associated with a higher age range; yes, it was different! The children's work developed a degree of sophistication not encountered in school and this undoubtedly helped the children to develop some confidence. The school-based teacher wrote on one child's assessment card, 'It was very important for E . . . to have experienced the success the project brought him. Success is not something he associates very often with school.' A useful point? The use of resources external to the school

own terms. 'COLOUR AS LANGUAGE' did encourage each child to draw on his or her own strengths and to accept a variety of stimuli in their own terms. The edge was taken off any competitiveness because the focus was on the individual child experimenting and building on that experimentation to develop his or her own visual language. A small Vietnamese girl very definitely felt that this is what had happened for her, although she expressed it very differently! 'COLOUR AS LANGUAGE' set out to encourage confidence in art practice. It was, therefore, extremely important that at no stage should any child feel that the task was too difficult, or indeed inappropriate to him or her. We worked as a team, as well as attempting through art to

necessarily involves a meeting of different contexts, a sharing of ideas, a stretching of our accepted methods of work, a revising of structured objectives, the taking of some mutually calculated risks. All of these are essential to teaching which is alive to the possibility of growth — even from "unexpected sources".

Note: This report was written by a participating tutor and not an independent observer. Sustained research into this kind of work is going on in galleries and museums throughout the country, however, which should ensure that claims for it which are made in good faith are borne out in the longer term.
Editor.

32. Curriculum development groups

Initial teacher training can serve only as an introduction to what is a highly skilled and demanding career and will hardly support forty years' work in schools.

Support agents already identified in this document have been *head-teachers*, prepared to involve teachers in discussion about policy and ready to encourage experiment with strategies to implement it, *other teachers in the school* who may offer examples of good or bad practice as a basis for comparison with one's own work; and *local authority advisers* and others who provide in-service courses. Curriculum development often requires new working relationships, periods of experimentation, risk-taking, questioning and revaluing, and implies a

that both philosophy and practice can be reconsidered and revised. It is valuable in setting up a group to involve teachers from a number of schools to assist comparison with the experience and views of others from a different school. This may enable one to understand one's own situation more clearly.

It should, however, be understood that it is not only teachers who have a contribution to make in this case. Other people, either with a professional or personal interest in art, craft or design might be invited to join curriculum development groups to assist teachers to think more fully about their work. The influence of non-teachers and the value of their involvement should not be underestimated. Non-teachers can act as catalysts enabling teachers to confront ideas and possibilities derived from

preparedness to work for and accept an inevitable degree of change. Most of the time, relationships and practices within schools tend to encourage consolidation and work against dealing with change. Opportunities to consider curriculum change are provided through in-service courses, but their effect may only be inspirational and transitory. There is a need for a longer term, low-key, yet strongly-focused mechanism to support teachers' involvement in curriculum development.

Curriculum development groups provide an opportunity for refreshment and regeneration, where teachers make contact with colleagues involved in similar work and can share ideas from their own experience. These ideas can be evaluated and compared with those gleaned from other sources, so

experience different from that which schools can offer. This engenders a preparedness to deal with unfamiliar areas of study and a need to explain educational ideas and practices in a way that non-teachers can understand.

It is important that all members of a group are working members, and that *the basis for involvement is a willingness to learn from experience and to share that experience so that others may learn too.* The strength of any curriculum development group lies in the preparedness of the members to experiment, to report on their work, to evaluate it and to document it so that the results may be disseminated and implemented in schools.

Each member needs to recognise the value of his or her experience and expertise. This, for teachers, will lie in their knowledge of learning and teaching methods; for non-teachers, this will probably be derived from an involvement in art, craft or design. The value which members place on the various contributions will be significant in the way a group develops. A probationer teacher and an older teacher with over twenty years' experience will each have a contribution to make derived from their own experience and, of course, a teacher's contribution will be very different from that of a non-teacher.

Setting up a Group

The setting up of a curriculum development group can follow an in-service course. Through this, contacts will have been made with other schools and teachers will have begun to develop a shared vocabulary which enables them to reflect on their experience and discuss it. Groups need to begin in a modest way and gradually to build up experience and strength through the interest and commitment of their members. For some groups, preparation of materials or the formulation of guidelines stimulate their formation. But a group will probably be short-lived unless these are tested out in schools in different situations and the results evaluated by the group as a basis for deciding on future work. A group must refine and develop such materials and guidelines, putting them into practice and modifying them for its own purposes. There can be lots of wasted effort in preparing detailed and attractive materials which may have limited use and application in schools, or comprehensive guidelines which may only be half-understood or wrongly interpreted and poorly implemented.

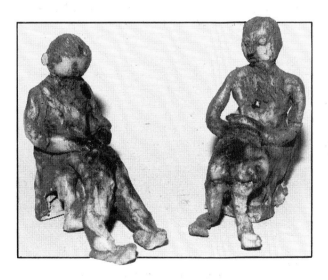

Development of a Group

The patterns of meetings will vary from group to group, but two meetings each term are probably the minimum — one to plan activities and one to report on what has been achieved.

Sub-groups may have to be formed, to deal with the various aspects of the dissemination process, and where possible the LEA adviser needs to be involved. The emphasis will be on consolidation rather than experiment, reflection rather than innovation.

Teachers will be expected to view their work critically and be prepared to explain and justify their ideas and practices in educational terms.

In art, craft and design education, it has become increasingly evident that work cannot be assessed on the evidence of products alone, but needs to take account of the growing experience and the changing and developing understandings of the people involved. Groups present similar problems. Their

success should not be measured in terms of the booklets they produce or the exhibitions they mount, but in terms of the way they encourage teachers to develop their work in schools and influence the school curriculum.

Curriculum development groups provide the mechanism to enable new ideas and practices to become more widely known and adopted by a greater number of schools and teachers so that what is initially innovation results in curriculum development through being absorbed into teachers' practice generally.

33. A primary/secondary arts working party

(Supporting art in local primary schools)
What follows is a description of how the head of an art and design department in a large secondary school initiated help in the teaching of creative arts for local primary schools. It demonstrates the value of such a subject specialist whose enthusiasm is used as an inspiration for motivating positive action, in a curriculum sense, while he and his staff become invaluable resource persons. Readers intent upon initiating similar courses of action should find it very useful as a preliminary guide. He writes:
The school in which I teach is an 11-16 comprehensive which is situated in a rural county and takes its pupils from eleven feeder primary schools within a radius of approximately twelve miles. The majority of these schools have under 100 pupils on roll and serve small rural villages. Communications for both pupils and teachers across the area and between primary and secondary sectors requires particular attention. The usual concerns about primary/secondary transition are amplified as in the insular, professional existence of many teachers in small, sometimes remote, village schools. For the anticipated benefit of both teachers and pupils it was my hope to improve the situation by proposing that a group of local teachers should meet on a regular basis in order to improve the effectiveness of Art in Education.

The Mechanics

To strengthen communications between schools and to highlight the role of art in education I believed it to be worthwhile to organise a series of meetings and activities for interested teachers. It was also my hope to encourage visits of primary pupils into the secondary school. Teachers in all feeder primary schools would be invited and emphasis would be placed upon each school sending at least one representative. The proposed group was to be called 'The Primary/Secondary Arts Working Party'.
If proposed meetings were to be effective, it was crucial that the mechanics were ironed out prior to circulation of my proposals. Hence the problems of teachers attending out-of-school meetings from a wide geographical area had to be solved with the agreement of the LEA. The following had to be provided:
  i) travelling expenses for teachers attending meetings
 ii) supply cover for teachers involved in the group's activities during school time.
The LEA and Advisory Service were approached and I set out in as much detail as possible the intentions of the group in writing. Their support was unanimous and strong.
I believed that the Working Party's aims and intentions should be stated clearly, and that details of the intended venue and the composition and

frequency of meetings should be circulated well in advance of the first meeting. The aims needed to point out the benefits for pupils as well as any possible contributions to INSET work which might develop from the group's activities.

Aims

— to facilitate the transition of pupils from primary to secondary school

— to increase interest and effectiveness of arts/crafts teaching in schools

— to offer further opportunities for teachers from remote schools to meet on professional terms

and were set out as:

1. For one teacher representative from each primary school to be an active member of the group.
2. To make the arts a more effective vehicle in aiding the children's objective understanding of the world in which they live through direct experience and personal involvement.
3. To provide a venue for primary school teachers to meet with each other thereby creating an arena to facilitate discussion regarding the purpose and function of the arts in primary education.
4. To establish the needs of, and possible support available to, primary schools, their teachers and their pupils.
5. To widen the strategies employed in the teaching of the arts by extending the perspectives from which ideas can be drawn.
6. By pooling resources to make the use of external agencies more accessible and viable, eg, Arts Council financial support, county advisory service, local Arts Centres.
7. To widen the specialist facilities and expertise to all primary schools in addition to their normal work.
8. To build a platform from which local schools can make demands upon the community in order to make their activities known to a wider public audience.
9. To aid problems of transition between primary and secondary schools.
10. To make available publications, papers, resources originating from other sources.

There was no desire to prescribe what or how primary schools should approach the teaching of the arts within the curriculum, and it was not the intention of the teachers at the Secondary School to direct or control the meetings. They were seen as coordinators and, in some instances, catalysts in specialist areas of demand.

Meetings

Although aims and purpose needed to be outlined for the first meeting it was also imperative to discuss them in concrete terms. It was essential, therefore, to establish a positive atmosphere and to structure the first meeting in order to discuss not only what may be achieved in the long term but more importantly what activities could be implemented in the immediate future. This approach would require the group to recognise the role of members as both consumers and contributors to group activities. Clear minutes needed to be taken not only for distribution to those participating but also to schools who were not represented, in the hope that they might be drawn into the arena by way of interest in any seemingly valuable outcomes.

Outcomes

Although initial meetings were enthusiastically attended, meetings of the working party are now held on an annual basis. This meeting is now held primarily to organise the summer Arts workshops. Other channels of communication between primary and secondary schools have been established and are proving valuable for maintaining contact. The main

outcomes are described below, although these are not extensive I believe that once a contact has been established it will act as a springboard for future initiatives.

1) Primary Art Workshops have without doubt been the main success of the venture. They are well attended and are now accepted as being part and parcel of the primary/secondary transition arrangements. Approximately forty pupils from different village schools attend each workshop which lasts for three hours. Three of four workshop sessions are required to satisfy the demand from the schools. During this time the pupils have the opportunity to work on simple art/craft projects directed by the art teachers in the secondary school. These are usually based upon direct observation, but encourage the pupils to move into media other than drawing and painting. Relief printmaking, simple ceramics or mixed media work are usually offered. Primary teachers are encouraged to attend and to assist, as indeed are parents of the visiting pupils. Very often it is the parents who provide transport and this is, therefore, a good opportunity for them to see the school during a normal working day. In addition to the workshops the pupils join in the normal morning break so they may experience as much of the school as possible. It has also been encouraging to welcome pupils from the local infant school who have attended their own Arts workshops at the comprehensive school (art, drama and music). Certainly a new perspective for the secondary teachers involved!

2) Primary schools should now know and understand that the art department is happy and willing to support them in activities within their own schools either by loaning specialist equipment or offering advice or help if and when required. Occasionally this facility has been used.

3) A number of primary teachers have a 'slightly improved' awareness of the comprehensive school and its staff, especially in the Arts department.

Time, distance and opportunity are still major pitfalls in trying to sustain long term and frequent contact between the art department and local primary schools. One of the most constraining limitations must be the amount of in-school time any one teacher can afford to divert to such ventures without causing unacceptable disruption to their regular classes and groups. Nevertheless contact between primary and secondary sectors at local level is worthy of our attention, especially if it highlights and helps to improve the effectiveness and value of art and craft work in the minds of both teachers and pupils.

The future?

Early in 1985 the teachers concerned with this venture met to consider possible ways in which it could develop. These included:

i) The holding of summer workshops for 4th year Junior pupils

ii) the extended use of specialist facilities to support work of primary schools

iii) the exploration of areas of the curriculum where co-operation may be established between primary and secondary school to ease the transition period

iv) the promotion of residential poet/playwright/writer meetings/courses — possibly financed by the Arts Council

v) the exhibiting of Primary art work in local hospitals

vi) the meeting of area exhibitions of work in schools

vii) the setting-up of a 'Data Bank'. Can we resource ourselves with material, reports, research, County projects, conferences and publications?

34. An outline structure used by the staff of one junior school for progression in art, craft and design education

This list — which is certainly not an extensive one — is provided as a guide so that primary teachers might consider the kinds of materials appropriate to their teaching in art, craft and design. Pupils should be introduced to various materials in stages so that they get to know and to use their qualities effectively and meaningfully in relation to curriculum experiences which the teacher plans carefully. It might be helpful, therefore, if children are encouraged to look at photographs, prints and slides of works of art to see how adult artists and craftpersons have used similar materials, for this will allow them to recognise techniques which they have either discovered for themselves or have been taught and to see new ones. In doing this they will be excited by the visual arts and their confidence will grow and strengthen.

1st Year Development

Functions

Description
Lots of close observational work - language plays an important part here. Pay attention to the development of good quality looking. Provide a wide variety of stimulus material.

Analysis
Selecting an area of interest. This provides material to use for 3D, textiles and printing. Introduce the use of simple focussing devices - magnifying glasses, viewfinders.

Communication
Visual storytelling. Step-by-step diagrams. Annotated drawings. Diagrams.

Problem-Solving
Introduce choices - ie. the background colour, paper, paper size. Working drawings, planning, sketching and colour tests.

Expression
Don't expect the children to do it all. Provide them with a start - a background for example. Consider multi-media pictures. Build up this kind of work in stages.

Skills

Drawing / Graphics / Design
Encourage confidence in one method. Show them what is available and what it can do and then let them choose. Use of pastels - oil, chalk etc. Pens - felt pens and pencils. Various papers - show how you select paper and media.

Painting / Picture Building
Lots of paint / colour mixing use of different brushes - choosing right brush for the job. Paint in stages - this avoids the disappointment of merging shapes and colours.

Printing / Collage
Handling printing inks + polyblock. Use of scissors and glue. Finger potato. crushed paper printing. String collage - print from this.

3D / Textiles
Simple clay / plasticine modelling pinch pots, impressed clay. Appliqué fabrics - glue and simple stitchery, couched threads. Simple card constructions.

2nd/3rd Year Development

Functions

Description	Skills
Description	**Drawing/Graphics/Design**
Continue observational work from a variety of sources and keep a close link with language work. Encourage looking for own stimulus and keeping a sketchbook. Pay attention to backgrounds now and use different viewpoints, light sources and distortions.	Scale of work - large v. small. Chalk & charcoal. Use of pencils different grades - explore and develop. Continue building confidence in the use of pastels
Analysis	**Painting/Picture Building**
Look at size and scale - magnify with and without viewfinders. Isolate interesting points and develop. Consider tone and colour.	Building a picture in layers. Use of a wash as a background small detailed work, small brush work.
Communication	**Printing/Collage**
Describing actions, conveying feelings, telling stories - look at the work of book illustrators.	Repeat patterns - paper and fabric. Collage from rubbings. Mixed media collage. Design specifically for printed work.
Problem-Solving	**3D/Textiles**
Problems in conveying 3D image. 3D constructions. Planning for printing using 2 colours or tones. Developing testers, samples, and colour tests.	Variety of fabrics & thread - built up work, mixed media foil and fabric. Weaving. Paper and card models. Moulded clay work. Rolling & cutting. Building with slabs. Decoration. Finishing & thickner Group work.
Expression	
Working from non-visual stimulus - music/poetry. Feelings through colour.	

3rd Year. Developments	Painting/Picture Building	Graphics/Design	Printing/Collage	3D/Textiles
Describing	Industrial landscapes.	Drawing all kinds of machinery and parts. Hand-held → automatic. Hammer & nails. Cheese grater. Pencil sharpener.	Foil collage. Mechanical patterns - repeating. Cogs & fitting together.	Pattern in foil & fabric.
Analysis	Metallic qualities - limited pallette to show rusty, shiny etc.	Working parts - large scale drawings. Clockwork mechanisms.	Print to show movement - push, pull, turn, spin, drag, lift (symbols for these?)	
Communication		Patterns for noises & movements - stop, start, breakdown. Action sequence - opening a tin, hammering a nail.		2D → 3D Montage - Time-Machine.
Problem-Solving		Design an extra pair of hands. Machine invention.	See also Animals & Machines: Movement a document by Peter Riches of Eggbuckland School.	Clay - industrial landscapes.
Expression	Roller skating. The factories take over the countryside.			Industry/Machines

4th Year Development	Painting/Picture Building	Graphics/Design	Printing/Collage	3D/Textiles
Describing	A Medieval Feast (Les Très Riches Heures) Bruegel's Harvest Still Life - Cézanne The Last Supper. A Meal in My House	Drawing fruit, vegetables grains.		
Analysis		Enlarge above studies – use as stimulus for printed/textile work.	Printing with hard fruits and vegetables.	
Communication	'Butter Mountain'	Advertising campaign - packets, adverts, magazine, TV (designing set to fit dialogue)		Clay 'bad fruits' with worms. Fruit surprises – instead of stones & pips there is —?
		Fat v. lean.		Inventing packaging for foods.
Problem Solving		Designing new eating/ food preparation tools.		
Expression	Fattypuffs & Thinifers.	Design clothing/jumpers for butchers, greengrocers etc.	Food Collage - My favourite meal.	

4th Year Development

Functions	Skills
Description Continued observational work. Careful choice of media and papers particularly shape and size. Economy of line, graphic accuracy. Living images. 5 minute sketches. **Analysis** Designing for other media - show how some images lend themselves to a particular media. Changes - metamorphosis and distortion. **Communication** Analysis of advertising images. Symbols & signs. Feelings. **Problem Solving** Planning for all work especially 3D constructions. Decision making group projects. **Expression** Developing a theme that is not immediately visual - emotions, inner self. Using collected images for imaginative work and building them into a composition. Illustrating literature - poems, fairy tales.	**Drawing/Graphics/Design** Drawing for information. Build on previous pencil work. Working in the environment - on location limited time projects. Develop sensitivity in choice of graphic materials - build on confidences, allow choices. **Paint/Picture Building** Building up expressive work. Observational painting - colour work important. Short painted sketches. Painting with objects other than brushes. **Printing/Collage** Designing for this purpose. Screen printing. Batik. Tie and dye. Printing for a purpose - tickets and posters. Collage using 2/3 media. **3D/Textiles** Fabric printing and embroidery. Putting ideas for clay into practice. Large models, figures etc.

7

MATERIALS

Painting Materials

Paints

- *Powder colours* are quite strong and bright when mixed with water. They may be diluted to produce broad 'washes'
- *Colours blocks* are concentrated cakes of hard powder colour which are clean and economical but are not recommended for general use. They are ideal for making thin 'washes' but not for producing thick, strong colours and are very hard on brushes
- *Ready-mixed colours* are brilliant poster-like paint produced in squeezy bottles or in tubs. They maybe thinned with water or used very thickly indeed
- *Water-colours* These come as small tablets or tubes of colour in metal boxes and are used to produce transparent washes
- *Finger paints* P.V.A. medium may be added to these colours if a richer texture is required and will render them waterproof. Mono printing can be improved if ordinary washing-up liquid is added as a medium

  A basic range of colours consists of:

	suggested qty
● White	3
● Black	3
● Red	1
● Yellow (lemon & brilliant)	2
● Blue (cobalt & prussian)	1

  is all that is needed to give young children experience of colour mixing and painting. As they develop, however, other colours (*emerald green, burnt umber, violet,* etc) can be added

Painting implements

- Hands and fingers
- Sticks
- Rags
- Card
- Brushes — stiff hog-hair type; soft water-colour type
- Plastic spatulas
- Palette knives

Palettes

- Formica off-cuts
- White card or paper
- Plastic or glass pots (discarded from the kitchen)
- Old saucers or plates

Printing Materials

Inks

- Non-waterproof (water-based) inks obtainable from an art materials supplier
- Various paints — particularly ready-mix colours
- Gelmix to thicken paint
- Various inks — both waterproof and non-waterproof (black, white and a range of colours)
- Dyes for use on paper or fabric

Rollers

- A selection of rubber-covered rollers (2", 3" and 4")

Inking-up slab

- A piece of white formica or hardboard
- A piece of plastic on a table top
- White paper or card
- A strong glass slab

Papers

- Newspaper (for experimental work)
- Newsprint
- Butcher's paper
- Typing paper (Experiment with white, black or coloured papers of all kinds)

Drying rack

- A string with paper clips or pegs to hold prints as they dry

Drawing Materials

Crayons
- *wax crayons* are soft and useful on various papers. They are useful for large-scale sketching as well as for making rubbings of textured surfaces. It is possible to scratch drawings through crayonning, in black, white or colour
- *conté crayons* enable children to draw sharp lines and various tones in black, white or terra-cotta on white or coloured sugar and craft papers

Charcoal
- a soft, tonal medium which will require fixing with a sprayed-on fixative (using diffuser or aerosol)

Chalk
- another but rather harder, tonal material than charcoal which can be applied to coloured, white or black card and paper

Pencils
- those in the 'B' range (B-6B) offer useful black and grey tonal qualities for mark-making
- those in the 'H' range (H-4H) may be used for fine or delicate line drawing but are not of great benefit to younger children
- coloured pencils lend themselves well to experimentation

Charcoal pencils
- these range from soft to hard in quality and take the form of pencils or paper-covered charcoal sticks

Inks
- black (for work on white or light-coloured paper or card)
- white (for use on dark grey or black paper)
- coloured (all may be used with pens and brushes and water may be added for the non-waterproof variety to produce useful, print only tonal qualities)

Colour sticks
- these produce subtle, gentle colouring and are especially effective on dark paper

Felt-tipped pens
- large black markers are very effective for bold work on a large scale

Fibre-tipped pens
- small-point pens may be useful for delicate drawing and sketching
- coloured pens permit children to produce painterly-like drawings but it is sometimes wise to restrict the range of colours, ie black and greens; black and browns; black, yellows and browns
- metallic coloured markers

Ball-point pens
- black and various colours can be of considerable help when children are producing detailed drawings

Oil pastels
- these are expensive and are soon used up. They produce drawings of a soft, beautifully-seductive quality which will add a new dimension to the children's drawing experiences

Adhesives

- **P.V.A. Medium:**
  A Poly Vinyl Acetate solution of plastic-like particles in water which is white. The water evaporates leaving a mouldless transparent plastic film.
  Can be used directly from the bottle giving a strong bonding adhesive. If diluted with various amounts of water, an adhesive of different strengths is produced which can then be used more economically for different applications on most surfaces
  It can be used as a painting medium for if mixed with water-based paint it produces a gloss finish. (Clean brushes thoroughly immediately after use). P.V.A. may be mixed with sawdust, sand, grit, etc, for collage work to obtain interesting textures. (Marvin Medium, Handcraft P.V.A. etc.). It can also be mixed with water and be used as a clear varnish or for stiffening fabric.

- **Araldite:**
  A powerful epoxy resin adhesive which is resistant to almost all solvents. (Twin tube pack) Used in joining metals to stone, etc, and can therefore be used in jewellery and sculpture.

- **Britfix:**
  A quick-drying waterproof, transparent cement for Balsa wood, soft and hard woods, plastic and leather.

- **Blu-tack:**
  Adhesive putty for fastening drawings (except on emulsion painted surfaces), charts and pictures to walls. It can be re-used and leaves no marks.

- **Copydex:**
  This white, latex paste gives a flexible bond between most materials. It is soluble in water before it dries and is used mainly on fabrics and lightweight materials — can be thinned slightly with water.

- **Clear Gum:**
  Non-staining and water-soluble for use with paper. (It may be washed out of clothes.)

- **Cellulose Powder:**
  When mixed with water this produces a low cost paper adhesive or can be added to paint. Useful for large sheets of paper, papier maché and finger painting.

Paper/Boards

- Sizes   mm   ins
    - AO 840 × 1189   33.11 × 46.81
    - A1 594 × 841   23.39 × 33.11
    - A2 420 × 594   16.54 × 23.39
    - A3 297 × 420   11.69 × 16.54
    - A4 210 × 297   8.27 × 11.69 the standard size of typing paper
    - A5 148 × 210   5.83 × 8.27

Cardboard
- Thin cards (3-sheet) make an ideal, flat mounting card or, in display, will take transfer or hand lettering and will roll easily. (Suitable for use in 3-D forms.) Thick cards (6 or 8 sheet) are excellent for modelling and constructional techniques (more rigid)

Mounting Boards
- Strong, thick, coloured boards suitable for mounting work

Greyboard
- This type of board is useful for model-making and book binding

Cartridge (Lightweight)
- Ideal for primary activities, including the use of water-based paints, drawing inks, etc

Cartridge (Mediumweight)
- Suitable for all types of drawing (pen and ink, water-based paints, pastels and crayons) and for paper sculpture

Cellophane
- Clear and coloured is ideal for transparent colour work in primary schools (useful for display and collage)

Corrugated Cardboard Rolls
- Corrugated card is ideal for backdrops as well as model making, display work and partitioning of classrooms

Cover Paper
- A high quality, heavyweight paper (suited to display, but also useful in printing work)

Crêpe Paper
- Most useful for display, collage, decorations and paper flowers

Draughting Paper
- Is useful for large scale work. The square paper can be used most successfully when sectional work on large murals is envisaged

Freize Papers
- Useful for cut paperwork, mounting and display (suitable for work with chalk, pastels, crayons, etc; pattern making, printing and decorative uses)

Kitchen Paper
- Cheap (a substitute for newsprint) Highly absorbent but tends to disintegrate with excessive wetting

Newsprint
- Inexpensive paper for experimental and practice work

Poster Papers
- Useful papers for printing purposes (prints taken from all blocks — lino, string, card, etc, look well on these coloured backgrounds). In the smaller sizes, the paper is ideal for collage work

Poster Paper Roll
- Suitable for all forms of display, printing and decoration (coloured, one side only) yellow, light blue, gold, brown, black, orange, leaf green, grey, red, blue

Sugar Paper
- Varies in quality and thickness (standard and heavier grade available in a variety of colours including grey, black and white), with a durable, rough surface which tends to fade; *probably the best for painting due to its absorbent quality*

Tissue Paper
- Good for print-making, collage, freizes, etc; can be used folded and crumpled to make figures; and is useful in model making

Water Colour Paper
- A high quality, acid-free water colour paper (rough surface, ideal for water colours and drawing)

Printing Paper
- A soft absorbent paper specially good for all types of print work

Disco or Activity paper
- A range of bright colours for display, collage activities and decorative cut-paper work

Modelling Materials

Plasticine
- difficult to keep colours separated

Clay
- This is useful as a modelling medium and for

(terra-cotta)
(buff)
use in pottery
—dig it up in the school grounds, prepare and use it
—obtain it from your *Schools Supply Department* or Specialist Supplier
(Art Advisers will provide you with advice on the purchase, preparation and use of these materials)

Worktops
- hardboard or formica off-cuts to cover desks
- plastic sheeting

Tools
- fingers and hands
- sticks
- modelling tools
- sponges
- spatulas

Construction Materials

- bricks
- stones
- clay
- wood
- metal
- plaster
- units in various materials

Useful for expressive 3D work and for building models and exploring principles

Carving Materials

- wood
- stone
- plaster
- soap
- wax
- fire clay

Useful for cutting into, scraping, scratching and filing

Weaving Materials

- fibres
- string
- wool
- cotton
- raffia
- sisal
- wire (man-made fibres)
- filaments
- dyes
- metal foils
- cellophanes
- crepe paper

Useful for inventive work in weaving and knitting

BIBLIOGRAPHY

BIBLIOGRAPHY

Adams, E & Ward C, *Art and the Built Environment*, Longman/Schools Council, 1982

Adams E & Baynes K, *Art and the Built Environment Study Activities*, Longman/Schools Council, 1982

Allison B, 'Sequential Programming in Art Education' in Piper D W *Readings in Art & Design Education After Hornsey Lund Davis Poynter*, 1973

Allison B, "Identifying the Core in Art and Design" in *Journal of Art & Design Education* Vol 1 No 1 pp 55-66, 1982

Assessment of Performance Unit, *Aesthetic Development*, APU, 1983

Art Advisers Association, *Learning through Drawing*, A.A.A.,1968

Barrett M, Art Education: *A Strategy for Course Design*, Heineman, 1979

Baynes, *About Design*, Design Council, 1976

Best D "Free Expression in the Teaching of Techniques?" in *The British Journal of Educational Studies* Vol xxvii No 3, 1979

Brittain W L, *Creativity and the Young Child*, Collier Macmillan, 1979

Buber M, *Between Man & Man*, Macmillan, 1978

Calouste Gulbenkian Foundation, *The Arts in Schools: Principles, Practice and Provision*, Calouste Gulbenkian, 1982

Clement Robert, *The Art Teacher's Handbook*, Hutchinson, 1986

Cotton A & Haddon F, *Learning and Teaching Through Art and Crafts*, Batsford, 1974

Dean J, *Art and Crafts in the Primary School Today*, Black, 1963

D.E.S., *Primary Education in England*. A survey by H N Inspectors of Schools, HMSO, 1978

D.E.S., *Art in Junior Education*, HMSO, 1978

D.E.S., *The Curriculum from 5-16*, (Curriculum Matters 2), HMSO, 1985 (paras 33-38)

Design Council Report, *Design Education at Secondary Level*, 1980, p4

Eisner E W & Ecker D, *Readings in Art Education*, Blaisdell, 1966

Eisner E W, *Education Artistic Vision*, Macmillan, 1972

Eisner E W, *The Art of Educational Evaluation, A Personal View*, Flamer, 1985

Eisner E W, *The Art of Educational Evaluation*, Falmer Press, 1985

Field D & Newick J (Eds), *The Study of Education and Art*, Routledge, 1973

Figg G, 'In Search of a Curriculum Model for the Primary Schools' (pp 35-51) Journal of Art and Design Education Vol 4 No 1, 1985

Gentle K, 'The Development of Children's Art" in *Education 3-13*, Vol 9 No2, 1981

Gentle K, *Children and Art Teaching*, Croom Helm, 1985

I.L.E.A., *Clay* — Clay in the classroom: I.L.E.A., 1982 Children with Clay (seven booklets)
1. Introducing children to clay
2. Using the bulk of the clay
3. Marking the surface of the clay
4. Working from flat pieces of clay
5. Banging and carving clay
6. Working from rolls of clay
7. Working with clay and fire
All published for the Inner London Education Authority by I.L.E.A. Learning Materials Service. Distributed outside I.L.E.A. by The Fulham Pottery Ltd
Learning to Look, 1981
Looking, 1981
Starting, 1981

Jameson K, *Junior School Art*, Studio Vista, 1971

Jameson K, *Pre-School and Infant Art*, Studio Vista, 1968

Lancaster J, 'The Artist looks at the School Environment,' Froebel J, 1971

Laxton M, *Using Constructional Materials*, Van Nostrand Reinhold Co (for the Schools Council, London)

Macdonald S, *The History and Philosophy of Art Education*, U.C.P., 1970

Marcousé R, *Using Objects*, Van Nostrand, 1974

Marshall S, *An Experiment in Education*, C.U.P., 1963

McFee J K & Degge R, *Art Culture and Environment* (see section on objectives pp372-380), Wadsworth 1977

McGregor R N, 'Building your own Art Curriculum Kit' (In Studies in Design Education & Crafts Technology, Col 11 No1), Winter, 1978

Mid Glamorgan Education Committee, *An Approach to Art in the Primary School*, 1984

Pickering J, *Visual Education in the Primary School*, Batsford, 1971

Read H, *Education Through Art*, Faber, 1958

Richardson M, *Art and the Child*, U.L.P.,1948

Robertson S, *Rose Garden and Labyrinth*, R.K.P., 1963

Robertson S, *Creative Crafts in Education*, R.K.P., 1963

Robertson S, *Using Natural Materials*, Van Nostrand, 1974

Ross M, *The Creative Arts*, Heineman, 1978

Schools Council, *Working paper 26 — Education through the use of materials,* Evans/Methuen, 1969
Design for Today, Edward Arnold, 1974
Materials and Design: A fresh approach, Edward Arnold, 1974
Education through Design and Craft, Edward Arnold, 1975
Children's Growth through Creative Experience, Van Nostrand, 1976
Art 7-11, 1978
Resources for Visual Education 7-13, 1981
Working Paper 75 — Primary Practice, Methuen, 1983

Scriven M, *The Methodology of Education* (AERA MONO, series on Curriculum Innovation), Rand McNally, 1967

Sharples D E, 'Three-Dimensional Work in The Primary School,' (pp 53-60), Journal of Art and Design Education Vol 4 No1, 1985

Southworth G, *The Curriculum Process Model and Its Implications for Visual Education in the Primary School,* unpublished MEd thesis University of Liverpool, 1980

Southworth G, 'The Process of Teaching Art in Primary School' in *Education 3-13,* Vol 9 No 2, Autumn pp 25, 26, 1980

Suffolk County Council, *Art 4-11,* Suffolk and Berol, 1985

Taylor Rod, *Educating for Art: Critical response and development,* Longman, 1986

Williams P H M, *Teaching Craft, Design and Technology Five to Thirteen,* Croom Helm, 1985

Witkin R, *The Intelligence of Feeling,* Heinemann Educational Books Ltd, 1974

NATIONAL SOCIETY FOR EDUCATION IN ART & DESIGN

What is the NSEAD?

The *National Society for Education in Art and Design* is the leading national authority combining professional subject association and trade union functions, which represents every facet of art, craft and design in education. Its authority is partly based upon a century-long concern for the subject, established contacts within government and local authority departments, and a breadth of membership drawn from every sector of education from the primary schools to universities.

The unique membership position of the Society makes it the only educational organisation which is able to draw on opinions of practising experts and to promote policies for, and on behalf of, all sectors of education in one specific subject area.

The NSEAD's roots can be traced to 1888, when a group of art school principals, who felt the need to raise the standard of art teaching and improve the status of art teachers, founded the *Society of Art Masters*. With the development of art and crafts as part of general education, and the appointment of men and women as full-time specialist teachers in schools, the membership was extended and in 1944, the Society adopted the title of *The National Society for Art Education*.

Another strand of the Society's history concerns the *Society for Education Through Art* which grew out of the framework of an art research institute for exploring new ideas in art and education, proposed by Henry Moore, Eric Gill, Herbert Read and Alexander Barclay-Russell. The SEA itself was formed in 1940 by the amalgamation of the *Art Teachers' Guild* and the *New Society of Art Teachers*. After two years of negotiations the SEA and the NSAE merged their interests as the NSEAD in October 1984.

What does the NSEAD do?

The NSEAD has many contacts within government and local authority departments, and is thus able to offer guidance to those with responsibility for various aspects of art, craft and design education. The Society is officially recognised by the Department of Education and Science as a professional association through which negotiations on behalf of art, craft and design education are conducted.

The experience and expertise of the NSEAD within and around a specialist subject area provides strength in formulating and presenting policies for curriculum and professional development, and the conditions of service which are conducive to such growth.

The NSEAD promotes the policies of a continued, strong and recognisible sector of further and higher education concerned with art, craft and design education and the vigorous defence of the high international status of the subject at this educational level. The Society is equally committed to the policy, at primary and secondary school level, of strengthening the role of the arts in general education with a clear recognition of the unique contribution and central importance of the subject to the core curriculum. The NSEAD is deeply concerned that art, craft and design education, at all levels, should be mutually sustaining.

The NSEAD aims to safeguard the interest of members by providing legal advice and assistance in professional matters, and by offering substantial insurance benefits comparable to those offered by other organisations.

The NSEAD is a fully independent trade union; it is not affiliated to any other union, neither is it a member of the TUC. The Society greatly values this autonomy.

JOHN LANCASTER, ATD, MPhil, PhD, DAE, FSAE, has taught in schools, colleges and university — more recently as head of the unique 'transbinary' postgraduate art teacher training centre in Bristol. His higher degree research, pursued at the universities of Bristol and London, was concerned with (i) professional courses in art, craft and design in the training of primary teachers, and (ii) an examination of the history of specialist art teacher education in Bristol in relation to national trends. He has published widely in the fields of art, craft and art education as well as lecturing extensively in the USA, Norway and Africa.